INSPIRED BY NATURE

CHÂTEAU, GARDENS, AND ART OF CHAUMONT-SUR-LOIRE

EDITORIAL DIRECTOR
Suzanne Tise-Isoré
Style & Design Collection

EDITOR
Gwendoline Blanchard

TRANSLATOR
Charles Penwarden

DESIGN
Bernard Lagacé and Lysandre Le Cléac'h

COPYEDITING AND PROOFREADING
Lindsay Porter

PRODUCTION
Élodie Conjat

COLOR SEPARATION
Les Artisans du Regard, Paris

Printed in Spain by Indice

With the authorization and participation of the
Domaine régional de Chaumont-sur-Loire.

Simultaneously published in French as
Château de Chaumont-sur-Loire.
Art et jardins dans un joyau de la Renaissance.
© Flammarion, S.A., Paris, 2019

English-language edition
© Flammarion, S.A., Paris, 2019

19 20 21 3 2 1

ISBN: 978-2-08-020350-2

Legal Deposit: 02/2019

INSPIRED BY NATURE

CHÂTEAU, GARDENS, AND ART OF CHAUMONT-SUR-LOIRE

Text CHANTAL COLLEU-DUMOND   Photography ERIC SANDER

Flammarion

CONTENTS

6   Preface by Bernard Faivre d'Arcier
9   Preface by Coline Serreau
10 Foreword

15 **A CHÂTEAU REVITALIZED**
16 Introduction
19 Milestones
22 The Chaumont-Amboise Family
24 The Porcupine
26 Catherine de' Medici
29 The Ruggieri or Astrologer's Room
32 The Catherine de' Medici Room
37 The Council Chamber
43 An Outstanding Collection of Tapestries
46 Diane de Poitiers
49 The Guard Room
50 The Grand Staircase
52 The Dining Room
57 Germaine de Staël
58 The Library
61 The Little Living Room
62 The Billiards Room
64 Marie-Charlotte-Constance Say
67 The Great Salon
71 The Nini Medallions
73 The Maharaja Jagatjit Singh of Kapurthala
76 The Grisailles
81 The Stables

BELOW Panoramic view of the château of Chaumont-sur-Loire from its historic park.

89 **A KALEIDOSCOPE OF GARDENS**
91 Introduction
94 **The Parks**
95 The Historic Park
101 The Ice Store
103 Prés du Goualoup Park
106 **The International Garden Festival**
113 The Power of Multidisciplinarity
118 The Ephemeral Gardens
127 "Extraordinary Gardens, Collectors' Gardens"
133 "Flower Power"
136 "Gardens of the Deadly Sins"
141 "Gardens of Sensations"
144 "Gardens of Delight, Gardens of Delirium"
149 "Gardens of Color"
154 "Body and Soul Gardens"
158 Laboratory and Observatory
163 Spectacular Scenarios and Stagings
171 The Elements
174 Materials
183 New Techniques, New Cultures
187 Recycling and Recuperation
190 Innovative Ideas
195 Structures of All Kinds
200 Extraordinary Floors and Paths
205 Design
209 Botany
214 **A Multisensory Experience**
215 Colorful Gardens
221 Sound Gardens
225 Perfumed Gardens
226 Light and the Gardens at Night
231 Humor and Fantasy
234 A Fairytale World
239 Poetry
242 Green Cards
248 **A Protean Garden**
249 The Metamorphosis of an Estate
255 Interstitial Gardens and New Gardens

269 **CONTEMPORARY ART IN ARCHITECTURE AND LANDSCAPE**
270 Introduction
277 A Unique Experience of Art and Nature
282 A Poetic Utopia
289 Natural Materials
304 Circles and Spheres
309 The Triumph of Color
312 On Ecology

316 Index of Names, Artworks, and Gardens
318 Acknowledgments and Photographic Credits

PREFACE

This book reflects the development and prestige of the Domain of Chaumont-sur-Loire since 2008, which is when the château, the International Garden Festival, and the Centre d'Arts, created on the same occasion, were brought together under a new identity on the initiative of the Centre-Val-de-Loire Region, which had become the owner of this estate. For the Domain, this transfer from state to region opened a new chapter, enabling this somewhat forgotten château to raise its national and international profile. The doubling of visitor numbers over the last ten years is the sign of the public's growing enthusiasm for this very unusual cultural, artistic, and horticultural adventure.

Chaumont-sur-Loire is a unique place, where discipline and the desire for excellence and quality come together with hospitality and the joy of sharing art and poetry. Driven forward by the energy of its director, by the enthusiasm of its teams, and by the talent of the artists and landscape designers who have come here from all around the world, every year the estate rises to the challenge of transforming its gardens and artworks. The regional Domain of Chaumont-sur-Loire is an estate in motion, in a state of perpetual evolution.

Bernard Faivre d'Arcier
Chairman of the Board of Administration of the Domain of Chaumont-sur-Loire

FACING PAGE The château was built in the fifteenth century facing the Loire river, in order to benefit from what, until the nineteenth century, was one of the longest navigable arteries in France.

PREFACE

One winter's day, not long after I had settled in the little village in Loir-et-Cher that faces the château of Chaumont-sur-Loire, I met a very affable woman who came up to me and asked if by any chance I was Coline Serreau. And that is how I got to know my wonderful neighbor Chantal Colleu-Dumond.

After that, I discovered and witnessed the development of what she was building at Chaumont. Under her direction, as the years went by, the more you could feel the effect of her visual mastery, her good taste, and her kindly, intelligent, and rigorous leadership, turning the place into a little paradise.

Contemporary art is exhibited in Chaumont in accordance with a strict and uncompromising editorial line, whose beauty and precision are welcomed with enthusiasm. There is no empty posturing here, no flashiness. There are artists sensitive to their world, eager to speak to their contemporaries, and who do so with elegance and restraint, by magnifying nature and matter. The International Garden Festival presents both budding and confirmed artists. They create their gardens in accordance with a set theme that must inspire but not stifle them. The teams at Chaumont spare no effort, bending over backwards to advise, modify, improve, and bring each project to life and fruition, so that it will endure for the season while losing none of its character. What an endeavor! And what respect for the artists! The many and varied visitors know what they are doing. The Garden Festival is well and truly the annual event for lovers of miniature paradises. They come here looking for ideas, emotions, surprises, fragrances, and entire worlds.

And of course, the château, that jewel of our heritage, is resplendent under those majestic cedar boughs, who reach out to us like arms inviting us to compare the elegance of human constructions with that of nature's cathedrals as they rise up and defy gravity with such grace and ease. Without computers or technology, these giant cedars teach us humility, freedom, moderation, and equilibrium, values that presided over the construction of the châteaux along the Loire, all those years ago, in an age exhausted by war and desiring to live again.

And then, last but not least, there is in Chaumont what can be called the "interstices," that is to say, all the elements there that we do not call works of art but that envelop visitors in their discreet splendor.

And that is the work of a woman, of an eye, the work of a director: the walls of pink roses, the lingering perfumes, the lines of flowers in carefully conceived color codes positioned on the lawns, the wrought-iron borders, the trees, bushes, and shrubs positioned just so, as if by chance, the wild and free invented spaces where species mix, the ponds where frogs live, the teeming harmony that seems to have come about by chance, and the constant attention of the gardeners working to ensure that visitors will always be treated with the respect due to a prince. That is what Chaumont is to me: a place that one always leaves feeling happy, wanting to come back.

Coline Serreau
Filmmaker and member of the Académie des Beaux-arts

FACING PAGE The historic park created by Henri Duchêne features some trees of impressive size, such as the cedars planted by the Count d'Aramon in the mid-nineteenth century.

FOREWORD

After long years abroad serving art and culture, destiny brought me to Chaumont-sur-Loire, where an ambitious project was afoot, connecting art, history, and gardens. And the adventure proved so compelling that these last ten years have done nothing to diminish my enthusiasm for the work of promoting this extraordinary place. If the International Garden Festival was already very well known, the artistic side was virtually starting from scratch. Likewise, the possibilities for exploiting the fascinating but somewhat forgotten château were well-nigh boundless.

It is through this very rich and very complex universe that I was given the chance—and considerable freedom—to embellish year after year, that this book will guide you. To direct Chaumont-sur-Loire is to care for the soul of an estate; it is to watch over a perpetually metamorphosing paradise; it is to sustain a miracle and make sure that it lasts. It is also to conceive of a project as a whole, like a work of art. It is to initiate and accompany constant and fascinating artistic developments, while preserving the sensibility and the fragility of the stones and trees. It is to endlessly and seamlessly link past, present, and future.

Chaumont-sur-Loire is a living place because it is in phase with all the rhythms of life, nature, and the seasons; because permanent renewal and creativity seem to be written into its historical DNA.

This constant movement, this openness to the world, and this connection with the timeless beauty of the landscape, the architecture, and the gardens are one of the strengths of this place and no doubt part of its magnetic power over the imagination.

The château, the gardens, and the artworks are of a piece linked by a shared desire for harmony.

The very sensitive vision of Eric Sander, a remarkable photographer with a keen eye for the beauty of the world, who has been exploring the château, the grounds, and the gardens for many years now, subtly reflects this singular universe with a threefold identity that is the Domain of Chaumont-sur-Loire.

Chantal Colleu-Dumond
Director of the Domain de Chaumont-sur-Loire

FACING PAGE The fifteenth-century architecture of the château is juxtaposed with contemporary art to form a precious whole. In 2011 Sarkis installed his *Ailleurs, Ici* in this space.
PAGES 12–13 The *Fleurs fantômes* (2014–16) hung on the château wall by Gabriel Orozco were inspired by the wallpaper of the Prince and Princess de Broglie.

A CHÂTEAU REVITALIZED

INTRODUCTION

There is no other château quite like it. Its unique privilege is to be a true château standing on the banks of the Loire and looking out over a landscape of fields and forests that have lain virtually untouched for centuries. The views contemplated by today's visitors are similar to the scenery admired by Catherine de' Medici, Diane de Poitiers, or Germaine de Staël when they came to Chaumont-sur-Loire.

Time, too, has a distinctive quality here. This place appears, more than most, to be a concentrate of history, art, architecture, and gardens, one that has been constantly reborn and has reinvented itself over the ages. The château's towers and keep have an archetypal quality that visitors can dream on.

Its very "human" scale gives the edifice the feel of a large residence that it is easy to imagine living in. This singularity accounts for much of its charm.

It has to be said that Chaumont offers a marvelous illustration of what the French call *la vie de château*, with its interior decoration, the elegance of its furniture, its splendid hangings, its remarkable stained glass, and the luxury of its stables and carriages.

It offers extensive views of wide, sandy paths and perspectives over the river and copses of trees landscaped by Henri Duchêne (1841–1902), as well as some extraordinary cedars.

All of which makes visitors want to give themselves up to the joy of strolling around, to reliving childhood moments: the conversation between the sky, the earth, the river, and the château seems to have been going for ever. The charm of Chaumont is something that is felt more than it is articulated or defined.

THE LOIRE

First of all, there is the river. Wide, peaceful, dotted with islands of sand and shaded by willows, a refuge to myriad birds in their summer nests or resting on their journey to distant destinations. A short walk from the Domain, indeed, lies the Île de la Folie, a secret refuge that shelters thousands of terns, seagulls, and wagtails.

It is hard to imagine that this river, France's longest, remained navigable up to the middle of the nineteenth century, and that at the foot of the château passed boats laden with merchandise destined for the estuary at Nantes. Today, only a few picturesque, flat-bottomed *gabarres* still venture out onto the "royal river," so-called for the many castles found on its banks.

As it flowed past, so the Loire sculpted a magnificent cultural landscape, listed as a World Heritage Site by UNESCO, shaped by centuries of interaction between the river, the land it irrigates, and the inhabitants who have settled on its banks through the ages.

The Loire was a major channel of communication and trade up to the nineteenth century, lined with ports and levees designed to protect inhabitants and land whenever this wild river burst its banks.

The countryside has been sculpted by its flow, by the vines, the fruit and vegetable gardens, and the crops. The villages, farms, and towns scattered along its banks reflect the importance of its influence.

The medieval fortresses of the Loire Valley, a seat of royal power, were gradually transformed into palaces during the Renaissance. These were open to the landscape, with extraordinary panoramas and views over the surrounding countryside. At Chaumont, this has been happily saved from the unsightly excesses of misbegotten architecture.

FACING PAGE, TOP Paul-Ernest Sanson, *The Château of Chaumont-sur-Loire from the North Bank of the Loire*, watercolor, early twentieth century. Archives nationales, Paris.
FACING PAGE, BOTTOM The village and château of Chaumont-sur-Loire viewed from the opposite bank.

POVR L'AVENIR

MILESTONES

Chaumont-sur-Loire was built in 1000 by Eudes I (c. 950–c. 996), Count of Blois, as a fortress. Like all such lordly dwellings of the time, it was built high up where it could survey the frontier between the counties of Blois and Anjou. In 1054 the château passed into the hands of the Amboise family, where it remained for five centuries.

In 1465 the first château was burned down on the orders of Louis XI (1423–1483), who wanted to punish Pierre I d'Amboise (1408–1473) for his involvement in a plot against the monarchy. Not long afterwards, however, it was rebuilt by the Chaumont-Amboise family, by which time Pierre I was back in favor.

In 1550 Catherine de' Medici (1519–1589), the wife of Henry II of France (1519–1559), acquired the estate, which she used as a hunting lodge and a resting place on her journeys between the châteaux of Blois and Amboise.

She relinquished the château in 1560 as a concession to Diane de Poitiers (1499–1566), Henry II's favorite and her great rival at court, who had been made to return the Château de Chenonceau to the crown after the king's death. Diane now ordered the works that gave Chaumont the appearance we know today. In particular, her modernization completed the chemins de ronde of the gatehouse, or *châtelet*, and the Saint-Nicolas Tower. The masons also dotted their work with Diane's emblems of bows and quivers, hunting horns, and crescent moons.

In 1750 Jacques-Donatien Le Ray de Chaumont (1725–1803), Intendant of Les Invalides under Louis XVI, purchased the château and ordered the demolition of its north wing, thereby opening up a unique view over the Loire. He set up two factories, producing crystal and pottery, and brought in the Italian sculptor Jean-Baptiste Nini (1717–1786). Today Chaumont boasts the world's finest collection of medallions by this famous artist. Each piece is unique.

In 1833 the Count d'Aramon (1787–1847) acquired the estate and created a park. He was responsible for planting the cedars of Lebanon that can still be seen here today.

Restoration work began and continued with Viscount Walsh (1785–1860), who married d'Aramon's widow.

In 1875 the château was acquired by Marie-Charlotte-Constance Say (1857–1943), a very wealthy heiress. She was only seventeen and in the same year married Prince Henri-Amédée de Broglie (1849–1917). She decorated the rooms with Renaissance furniture and, with her spouse, supervised extensive renovation that would make their home worthy of the most splendid receptions. This work was entrusted to the architect Paul-Ernest Sanson (1836–1918), who also designed the luxurious stables. Finally, another architect, Marcel Boille (1850–1942), built the estate's model farm. In their time there, the Prince and Princess de Broglie welcomed most of the crowned heads of Europe and Asia to Chaumont-sur-Loire.

The Prince de Broglie, who had been a remarkable manager of the estate, died in 1917. At the age of seventy-three, the Princess de Broglie remarried. Her new husband was the Infante of Spain, Luis Fernando de Orleans y Borbón (1888–1945). The years that followed were marked by numerous financial difficulties that forced the princess to sell a number of her properties and to break up the estate at Chaumont, which now shrank from over six thousand to fifty-one acres.

In 1937 the French State started expropriation proceedings in the name of public utility. It took possession of the estate on August 1, 1938.

Having first been a national monument, the château became the property of the Centre-Val de Loire regional council in 2007.

FACING PAGE The coat of arms of the de Broglie family as it appears on the stable.

ABOVE On the façade of the stables, the intertwining double "C" of Charles II d'Amboise.
FACING PAGE The King's Room was so named in honor of Louis XII, who was invited to the château in 1503 by Georges d'Amboise, his first minister.

THE CHAUMONT-AMBOISE FAMILY

The Château de Chaumont as we see it today was built in the late fifteenth and early sixteenth centuries by the Chaumont-Amboise family, during a period of extraordinary architectural activity in the Loire Valley stimulated by the presence of the king and the court.

From 1468 to 1481 Pierre I d'Amboise and his son, Charles I (1430–1481), built the north wing facing the Loire (this no longer stands), the west wing, and the Amboise Tower, facing out toward the town of the same name.

The second wave of building work took place twenty years later, from 1498 to 1510, under the aegis of Charles II d'Amboise (1473–1511), helped by his uncle, the Cardinal Georges d'Amboise (1460–1510). They built the south wing, the gatehouse, the east wing, the Saint-Nicolas Tower, the grand staircase in the courtyard, and the chapel.

The Chaumont-Amboise family played an important role in the political and artistic history of France, and especially the youngest of their children, Georges, who was an eminent cleric. Born in Chaumont in 1460, he served Louis d'Orléans, the future Louis XII (1462–1515). After a series of prestigious ecclesiastical positions, he became the new king's first minister and helped ensure his popularity by his wise administration.

The Chaumont-Amboises were among the earliest and most important adopters of Italian styles in the French kingdom, helping set a trend that led the national elite to emulate the admired buildings across the Alps. Charles II d'Amboise, the son of Charles I, and his uncle Georges' favorite, was the first Frenchman to notice Leonardo da Vinci. He commissioned him to design a villa for his personal use and to execute paintings for Louis XII. In 1507, Georges was behind the famous artist's first trip to France.

ABOVE Coat of arms of Cardinal Georges d'Amboise on the façade of the main staircase.
RIGHT Jean Pichore, *Cardinal Georges d'Amboise behind Louis XII*, miniature from *Remedies for Fortune Fair and Foul* by Petrarch, 1503.
FACING PAGE Andrea Solario, *Portrait of Charles II d'Amboise*, oil on panel, early sixteenth century. Musée du Louvre, Paris.

THE PORCUPINE

The porcupine, a large representation of which adorns the fireplace in the Great Salon, was the emblem of Louis XII. It was originally chosen by his father, Charles d'Orléans (1394–1465), with the motto *Cominus et eminus*, meaning "from near and from afar." At the time, the porcupine was thought not only as being able to protect itself from attackers with its quills, but also as having the capacity to fire them at its adversaries like arrows. The motto was therefore a reference to the king's qualities of both clemency and severity.

ABOVE AND FACING PAGE The porcupine, the emblem of Louis XII and, before him, Charles d'Orléans, is found throughout the château. Here, it is seen in the Porcupine Room and on the mantelpiece of the Great Salon.

CATHERINE DE' MEDICI

Daughter of Lorenzo II de' Medici (1492–1519), Duke of Urbino, and Madeleine de la Tour d'Auvergne (1495–1519), Catherine de' Medici (1519–1589) grew up in Italy, where the death of her father and of her mother, only weeks after her birth, made her Duchess of Urbino. The death of her aunt, Anne d'Auvergne (c. 1495–1524), added the title of Countess d'Auvergne. The orphaned girl was raised in Florence and then in Rome under the direct protection of her uncle, Pope Clement VII (1478–1534). Gifted with a refined education, she was the sole heir of the Medici name and married Henry, brother of the dauphin, François III, Duke of Brittany (1518–1536). The early death of François III changed her destiny. As wife of the future Henry II, she became dauphine and Duchess of Brittany from 1536 to 1547, then Queen of France from 1547 to 1559. Mother of the kings Francis II, Charles IX, and Henry III, and of the queens Elizabeth (Queen of Spain) and Marguerite (known as "La Reine Margot," wife of the future Henry IV), she governed France as queen mother and regent from 1560 to 1563.

Catherine de' Medici is a major figure in sixteenth-century history. Although her name is associated with the wars of religion between Catholics and Protestants, she made diplomatic use of her influence in what was a complex and very turbulent period. She bought the château of Chaumont-sur-Loire in 1550, when she was just thirty.

It was, at the time, an attractive proposition: the château collected the taxes paid by merchants sailing their wares along the Loire and also possessed large tracts of agricultural land. Catherine used Chaumont-sur-Loire as a staging post between the châteaux of Amboise and Blois.

There is a chamber at Chaumont called the Ruggieri or Astrologer's Room. All her life, Catherine de' Medici employed the services of astrologers, the most famous of which were Luc Gauric (1476–1558), Nostradamus (1503–1566) and Cosimo Ruggieri (?–1615). She advocated a policy of conciliation and was behind the legislation granting freedom of conscience to Protestants. On numerous occasions, she spoke out for the idea of civil tolerance.

RIGHT Jacques de Broglie, *The Astrologer Ruggieri and Catherine de' Medici*, drawing, early twentieth century. Domain of Chaumont-sur-Loire.
FACING PAGE Santi di Tito, *Catherine de' Medici*, oil on canvas, late sixteenth century. Uffizi Gallery, Florence.

THE RUGGIERI OR ASTROLOGER'S ROOM

The so-called Ruggieri or Astrologer's Room in the Saint-Nicolas Tower was given this name by the château's last private owner, Marie-Charlotte-Constance Say. She dedicated the rooms on the second floor of the east wing in her residence to a museum recalling the figures who made their mark on its history.

The stone mantelpiece of the impressive polychrome fireplace in this room is engraved with mysterious signs, notably the Greek letter delta, which can be read as a kabalistic figure relating to astrology or as the initial of Diane de Poitiers. On the lintel, too, are three circles or three full moons. These can be deciphered as esoteric clues linked to the study of the stars or seen, once again, as an allusion to Diane de Poitiers, Diana being the goddess of the moon in Roman mythology.

According to legend, it was at Chaumont that Cosimo Ruggieri predicted to Catherine de' Medici the end of the Valois dynasty, to be replaced by the Bourbons, and the future of her three sons. Their three faces appeared successively in a mirror, each rotating the number of years they would reign as Francis II, Charles IX, and Henry III.

FACING PAGE The motifs adorning the lintel of the polychrome fireplace may be esoteric symbols or a simple allusion to one of the château's owners, Diane de Poitiers. RIGHT Unidentified artist, *Presumed Portrait of the Astrologer Cosimo Ruggieri (?–1615)*, oil on canvas, seventeenth century. Domain of Chaumont-sur-Loire.

ABOVE Detail of the decoration on a trunk in the Ruggieri Room.

THE CATHERINE DE' MEDICI ROOM

Originally a state bedroom, the Catherine de' Medici Room, the second room in the museum section of the residence of the Prince and Princess de Broglie, displays the oldest tapestry in the château collection. Woven in Tournai in the late fifteenth century, *The Story of Perseus and Pegasus* hangs close to a late sixteenth-century tapestry from Flanders, *The Story of David and Abigail*.

Recent acquisitions by the Domain recreate the atmosphere of the late nineteenth century, which was itself an attempt to evoke the bedroom of Catherine de' Medici, such was that period's reverence for the Renaissance. That is why we find here a remarkable four-poster bed in the style of Henry II—but from the nineteenth century—richly sculpted with plant figures, including garlands of leaves and fruits. Mermaids in half-relief, an amazon, and a warrior decorate its bedposts.

A sixteenth-century wedding chest with a convex top and panels separated by pilasters, bought by the Princess de Broglie, is another of the remarkable pieces of furniture recently put back into the bedchamber known colloquially as "Catherine's Room."

In the room can be seen a sixteenth-century throne decorated with an arch, underneath which is a heron swallowing an eel and two unicorns holding a shield. Nearby is a fifteenth-century armoire showing, on its top part, the three theological virtues—faith, hope, and charity—and the four seasons, while the lower part depicts the five senses. A full-length portrait of Catherine de' Medici, a nineteenth-century copy of an original painting in the Palatine Gallery at the Palazzo Pitti in Florence, decorates these apartments, along with a half-profile portrait of the queen in mourning, inspired by a painting by François Clouet (c. 1510–1572).

LEFT This detail of the chest placed at the foot of the bed in the Catherine de' Medici Room echoes the painting in the same space.
FACING PAGE Detail of *Catherine de' Medici*, oil on canvas, nineteenth century. The original, painted in 1556, is kept at the Palazzo Pitti in Florence.
PAGES 34–35 The Catherine de' Medici Room and *The Story of David and Abigail* tapestry, woven in the sixteenth century in Brussels.

THE COUNCIL CHAMBER

The Council Chamber is the château's state room. The Prince and Princess de Broglie took special care over its decoration and furnished it with some major pieces from their collection of artworks.

For example, they installed there an outstanding piece of seventeenth-century majolica from the Palazzo Collutio in Palermo, Sicily. This ceramic creation—comprising 1,938 faience tiles, which were taken apart and then reassembled one by one—depicts a hunting party surrounded by a fanciful border of acanthus scrolls populated by birds. Its blues, greens, and golds contribute to the beauty of this remarkable ensemble.

The Council Chamber at the Château of Chaumont-sur-Loire also displays a masterpiece of the art of tapestry from the late sixteenth century, *The Planets and Days* ensemble, which was recently restored in the workshops of the De Wit Royal Manufacturers in Belgium. Several years after being taken down, it was reinstalled in 2015.

The theme of this famous hanging is astrology. Each divinity of ancient Roman mythology—Diana, Saturn, Apollo, Venus, Mars, Mercury, Jupiter—corresponds to a day of the week and a planet and sits in a chariot symbolizing the movement of the stars. The wheels of each chariot contain one or several zodiac signs and each one is pulled by a fantastical or real animal associated with the divinity.

A tapestry from the same workshop, *Marriage*, with mythological scenes and bosky landscapes, was added to this extraordinary ensemble.

LEFT *Saccharumania* by Karine Bonneval,
installed in the Council Chamber in 2017.

AN OUTSTANDING COLLECTION OF TAPESTRIES

The Prince de Broglie furnished the château at Chaumont-sur-Loire with an outstanding ensemble of art objects from the fifteenth and sixteenth centuries. The French and Flemish tapestries, in particular, were chosen with great care, and now constitute one of the most prestigious collections of such artworks in the Loire Valley.

The château's oldest tapestry, hung in the Catherine de' Medici Room, was woven in Tournai in the late fifteenth century and is titled *The Story of Perseus and Pegasus*. Perseus, carrying a scythe and a shield, is averting his eyes from the petrifying gaze of Medusa, as he cuts off her head. Pegasus, the winged horse born of Zeus and Medusa, emerges from the blood pouring from the gorgon's neck. Next comes a singing contest with the nine muses, daughters of Zeus. Their music fills Mount Helicon with joy, causing it to swell and threaten to reach the heavens. Obeying the orders of Poseidon, Pegasus strikes the mountain with his hoof to make it go back to its usual size. In doing so, he causes a spring to burst forth. The source of poetic inspiration, it also witnessed the birth of the poet Orpheus.

The Story of David and Abigail, conceived in Brussels in the sixteenth century, is also exhibited in the queen's bedroom. It evokes the generosity of Abigail, who sent David provisions carried by donkeys to offset the insult inflicted by her cruel husband, the rich merchant Nabal, who sent David his soldiers instead of giving him food and drink.

A tapestry of *The Judgment of Paris*, made in Brussels in the sixteenth century, adorns the walls of the Dining Room. Paris, son of Priam, king of Troy, by Hecuba, was abandoned on Mount Ida. There he was raised by shepherds. He was ordered by Hermes to give the golden apple of discord to the most beautiful of the three goddesses he now saw before him: Hera, wife of Zeus; Athena, goddess of war; and Aphrodite, goddess of love. Seeking to sway his judgment, each of the goddesses made Paris a promise: Athena, who is shown wearing her armor, guaranteed him victory in war; Hera, who is followed by a peacock, offered sovereignty over men; and Aphrodite, who is accompanied by Eros and wears a heart necklace, offered him the love of the most beautiful woman in the world, Helen. Paris chose Helen, who happened to be the wife of Menelaus, king of Sparta. Paris took Helen away with him to Troy. The furious Menelaus formed an alliance with other Greek kings to destroy Troy and take back Helen, with the support of Athena and Hera. This was the beginning of the Trojan War.

The Story of Dido and Aeneas (Aubusson manufacture, seventeenth century) shows Dido, queen of Carthage, welcoming Aeneas, who arrives, wearing armor, on a cloud, after the fall of Troy.

The Library has a suite of tapestries depicting three episodes in the life of Alexander the Great: *The Triumphal Entrance of Alexander into the City of Babylon*, *The Submission of the Family of Darius*, and *The Meeting of Porus and Alexander*. They were woven in Aubusson in the seventeenth century, from cartoons by Charles Lebrun (1619–1690). The biggest of the three tapestries illustrates the arrival of the victorious Alexander, on a chariot pulled by an elephant, entering the city of Babylon, with its rich palaces and sumptuous hanging gardens.

The tapestry of *Ajax and Ulysses Fighting over the Arms of Achilles* (Brussels manufacture, sixteenth century) is exhibited in the vestibule. After the death of Achilles during the siege of Troy, Ajax and Ulysses fought over the warrior's arms. This tapestry shows the Greek armies, with the representation of the fleet particularly in evidence.

FACING PAGE Detail of *The Triumphal Entrance of Alexander into the City of Babylon*, woven in the seventeenth century in Aubusson.

Two episodes from the life of Hannibal, *The Fall of Saguntum* and *Hannibal Showing His Lieutenants the Plain of the Po*, are depicted on tapestries woven in the sixteenth century in Brussels, which hang in the Billiards Room. In the first tapestry we see Hannibal, leader of the Carthaginian army, launching the attack on Rome by taking Saguntum, an allied city. In the second tapestry the army, with its elephants, is completing its journey across the Alps, and Hannibal is rallying his men by pointing to the next stage of their journey—the plain of the River Po, the site of their next battle.

The *Planets and Days* tapestries constitute a priceless series. Recently restored, they are displayed in the Council Chamber, which was the château's state room. These remarkable hangings were woven in Brussels in the late sixteenth century by the master tapestry-maker Martin Reymbouts (1570–1619). This ensemble comprises eight tapestries, of which there are only two copies in the world—this one in Chaumont-sur-Loire and the other at the Bavarian National Museum in Munich. The tapestries were recently restored in the workshop of the royal manufacture at Wit in Belgium.

The series was listed as a historic monument in 1938, during the first inventory of the château. The main theme is astrology. In each of the tapestries, a Roman god sits in a chariot that symbolizes the movement of the stars, each one corresponding to a day of the week and to a planet. The chariots are pulled by animals, either real or imaginary, and emblematic of the god concerned. In the lower part of the tapestries are activities linked to the particular god, as well as mythological and biblical scenes depicted in woodland settings. The gods are recognizably Diana, Saturn, Apollo, Venus, Mars, Mercury, and Jupiter. Diana, the goddess of the moon, associated with the star sign Cancer, drives a chariot pulled by two dolphins. Saturn, god of time and agriculture, drives a chariot pulled by two dragons. Apollo, the god of the sun, oracles, medicine,. and the arts, who is associated with the star sign Leo and the day Sunday, drives a chariot pulled by four horses, symbolizing the four cardinal points. Venus, associated with Friday and the star signs Taurus and Libra, drives a chariot pulled by two doves, symbolizing purity and fidelity. Mars, the god of war, is associated with Tuesday (*Mardi*)— and his chariot is pulled by two wolves symbolizing the founding of Rome. The wheels show the zodiac signs of Aries and Scorpio. Mercury, the god of commerce, travelers, thieves, and the sciences, is associated with Wednesday (*Mercredi*). His chariot is pulled by two cockerels symbolizing the new day, while the wheels of the chariot display the signs of Gemini and Virgo. Jupiter is associated with Thursday (*Jeudi*). His chariot is pulled by two peacocks. The wheels of the chariot show the signs for Pisces and Sagittarius. At the feet of Jupiter is an eagle, the god's messenger.

Woven in the workshop of Martin Reymbouts, the *Marriage* tapestry completes this outstanding ensemble. Note the strong emphasis on plants in this piece, and in particular the luxuriant gardens.

FACING PAGE Detail of *The Story of David and Abigail*, woven in the sixteenth century in Brussels.

DIANE DE POITIERS

For more than twenty years, Diane de Poitiers (1500–1566) was the favorite of King Henry II, and therefore the rival of his legitimate wife, Catherine de' Medici. Combining keen intelligence with extraordinary beauty, gifted with an acute sense of politics and power, she exerted a strong influence over the king, who was very attached to her despite being twenty years her junior. Henry showered Diane with honors and gifts, entrusting his beloved with the crown jewels, and giving her a Parisian mansion, the Duchy of Étampes, and a hunting lodge at Clayes. Diane also received the royal property of Chenonceau and the revenues from the tax on *charges*, the prestige functions granted to courtiers, which were considerable. Finally, she was confirmed as the owner of land in Nogent, Anet, and Breval. After the death of Henry II, who was killed in a joust, the new king, Francis II, declined to sanction her, but she would no longer appear at court and, as was the custom, she had to return the crown jewels. Queen Catherine adopted a kindly attitude toward her and allowed her to enjoy the many gifts, possessions, and lands that had been granted to her by the king, her husband. Still, in late 1559 she compelled Diane to return the Château de Chenonceau, in exchange for which she gave her Chaumont early in 1560. Henry's former favorite now withdrew to Anet and made only sporadic stays at Chaumont. Nevertheless, she continued to take an interest in her other properties and kept building work going at Chaumont until her death in 1566, thus giving it most of the features we know today.

On inheriting the château, her daughter made plans to endow it with a park in 1573. She died the following year before they could be carried out.

LEFT Unidentified artist, School of Fontainebleau,
Diane de Poitiers as Diana the Huntress, oil on canvas,
sixteenth century. Musée de la Vénerie, Senlis.
FACING PAGE Unidentified artist, French school,
Diane de Poitiers, oil on canvas, sixteenth century.

THE GUARD ROOM

The Guard Room, located above the porch in the gatehouse, has always been, even in the times of the de Broglies, an ideal place for watching over the château, as it gives onto the drawbridge on one side and the courtyard on the other.

This room, which was once where the guards of the king or lord practiced the use of various weapons, had to be crossed by anyone going to the king's bedchamber.

This Guard Room features an exceptional strongbox made in the late sixteenth century in Nuremberg. Its function was to protect the charters, deeds of property, archives, and notarial documents of aristocratic families.

The chest has a remarkable lock, comprising twenty bolts and a highly complex mechanism, which provides extremely sophisticated protection with special combinations and makes it all but impossible to pick.

FACING PAGE This German strongbox from the late sixteenth century has a sophisticated lock mechanism comprising twenty bolts. RIGHT Detail of the suit of armor decorating the Guard Room.

THE GRAND STAIRCASE

The Grand Staircase, or Renaissance Staircase, was built in the 1500s. It is a spiral staircase set in a polygonal tower with windows on three sides. Its initial appearance was changed in the eighteenth century when the external gallery was built, and in the nineteenth century, with alterations to the roofing. It leads to the so-called "historic" apartments.

The windows are decorated with heraldic stained glass showing coats of arms made by the master glassmaker Georges Bardon (1846–1905) at the request of the Prince and Princess de Broglie. This stained glass refers to the successive owners of the Domain of Chaumont-sur-Loire, from the end of the first millennium (the Chaumont-Amboise family) to the late nineteenth century (the Aramon, Walsh, and de Broglie families). The external façade of the staircase was recently restored.

LEFT The Grand or Renaissance Staircase serves the historic apartments. The sculpted decoration combines both Gothic and Renaissance styles.
FACING PAGE The external façade of the Grand Staircase, decorated in a luxuriant, hybrid style.

THE DINING ROOM

This room is fifty-five feet (seventeen meters) long. Previously used solely by servants, it was converted into a dining room toward the end of the nineteenth century by the Prince and Princess de Broglie. Here we can detect the signature of architect Paul-Ernest Sanson. The fireplace of the Dining Room was conceived in the neo-Gothic style and was executed by the artist Antoine Margotin. On the mantelpiece there is the full repertoire of sculptural decoration noted on the château's external facades. There are, for example, the coats of arms of Charles I, who owned the château between 1468 and 1481, and of Charles II d'Amboise, who ordered the building works between 1498 and 1510. We may also recognize the coat of arms of Cardinal Georges d'Amboise. Other features are the Chaumont rebus depicting a mountain in flames, a visual pun that refers to the Chaumont name ("mont chaud") and the crest of the French royal family, both of which can be observed along the sides of this spectacular fireplace.

ABOVE Detail from the fireplace adorning the Dining Room.
FACING PAGE The grandly proportioned Dining Room on the ground floor of the south wing was laid out by the de Broglies.

ABOVE AND FACING PAGE This neo-Gothic fireplace was
designed by Paul-Ernest Sanson. Its sculptural decoration
recalls the arms of the previous owners: the coat
of arms of Georges d'Amboise is flanked by the double
"C" of Charles II d'Amboise.

GERMAINE DE STAËL

Germaine de Staël (1766–1817) stayed at the Château de Chaumont-sur-Loire in 1810, when her bold opposition to the Emperor Napoleon made her *persona non grata* in Paris. She was the guest of her friend James Le Ray de Chaumont (1760–1840) when he was away in the United States. While making plans to go into exile across the Atlantic, she agreed to move into Chaumont temporarily, where she could keep an eye on the publication of her book on Germany, *De l'Allemagne*, which would prove hugely influential. On the banks of the Loire she was joined by her circle of friends and intellectuals from around Europe, including Madame Récamier, Benjamin Constant, Wilhelm Schlegel, and Adelbert von Chamisso. They and others could be seen pacing the park and making the château echo with their debates and amorous quarrels. They stayed at de Staël's side from April to August 1810, until the owner of the château came back. In the end, Germaine de Staël abandoned her plans to leave for the United States herself. As for her book, it was banned and seized.

FACING PAGE Marie-Éléonore Godefroy, *Germaine Necker, Baronne de Staël-Holstein, known as Madame de Staël (1766–1817)*, oil on canvas, early nineteenth century. Châteaux de Versailles et de Trianon, Versailles.
RIGHT Unidentified artist, French School, *Madame de Staël Holding Forth*, lithograph, nineteenth century. Illustration for Charles d'Héricault's journal *La Révolution*, published in 1883.

THE LIBRARY

Originally a dining room, this room was transformed into a library by the de Broglie family. The princely couple also called it their "autumn salon." Sadly, the room was damaged by fire in 1957. It was then refitted with furniture from the Napoleon III period, including a particularly rare and original armchair called the "indiscreet," which allowed three people to converse together.

The large tapestry here represents *The Triumphal Entrance of Alexander into the City of Babylon*, while two others depict *The Meeting of Porus and Alexander* and *The Submission of the Family of Darius*.

ABOVE Detail of an Indian table rug, seventeenth century.
FACING PAGE The library was destroyed by fire in 1957. The room was recreated in 2007 with furniture similar to that of the de Broglies' time.

THE LITTLE LIVING ROOM

In the days of the Prince and Princess de Broglie, this room, which was destroyed by the fire of 1957, was used as a bedroom. Today it is a salon containing furniture of outstanding value, an ensemble that is itself a listed historical monument. It dates from the period when the writer Germaine de Staël was living at the château. The sofas, the armchairs, and the chairs are covered with gold leaf and upholstered in a style of green silk known as "lampas Hortense." This very precious furniture was executed by the famous cabinet-maker Pierre Benoît Marcion (1769–1840).

FACING PAGE Marie Denis, *Gold and Empire Herbarium*, exhibited in the Little Living Room in 2017.
RIGHT The Little Living Room is a homage to the writer Germaine de Staël, who stayed at the château in 1810.

THE BILLIARDS ROOM

In the de Broglies' day, this room was devoted to billiards, and therefore to exclusively male company. The men would also come here to smoke cigars and discuss politics after the dinners given by the princess.

Visitors can admire a magnificent polychrome ceiling from the nineteenth century with views of the château at the time and its Renaissance-style decoration. The tapestries, woven in Brussels during the fourth quarter of the sixteenth century, represent two episodes in the life of Hannibal: *The Fall of Saguntum* and *Hannibal Showing His Lieutenants the Plain of the Po*.

RIGHT Detail of the tapestry *Hannibal Showing His Lieutenants the Plain of the Po*.
FACING PAGE One of the late-sixteenth-century tapestries in the Billiards Room: *The Fall of Saguntum*.

MARIE-CHARLOTTE-CONSTANCE SAY

When the estate was acquired in March 1875 by Marie-Charlotte-Constance Say (1857–1943), heiress of the fortune from the Say refineries, the château was about to undergo a major evolution. That same year she married Prince Henri-Amédée de Broglie.

Her immense fortune, comparable to that of the Rothschilds—she also owned a townhouse in Rue de Solférino in Paris—enabled her both to develop the château and its park and to make it a remarkable place for entertaining; her lavish parties made it the epitome of the Belle Époque.

The prince and the princess called in the renowned architect Paul-Ernest Sanson, who brought modern comforts to the estate by equipping it with electricity and running water. He also designed the stables, now considered the finest in Europe. As for the park, the greatest landscape designer of the day, Henri Duchêne, was invited to restructure it.

Marie-Charlotte-Constance de Broglie, an eccentric and extravagantly colorful character, had a passion for receptions and riding to hounds.

At her château, she and her husband received many European monarchs, including Edward VII of England, Isabella II of Spain, Alfonso XIII of Spain, Charles I of Portugal, Carolus I of Romania, and Ahmad Shah Qajar, shah of Persia.

Passionate about the arts, and a musician, with a love of acting, she also invited many fashionable artists to her estate, among them Francis Poulenc, Sarah Bernhardt, and Marguerite Deval. She even had successful shows brought in from Paris by train, and never hesitated to invite actors from the Comédie-Française.

ABOVE Two photographs from unidentified photographers, *Prince Henri-Amédée de Broglie* (left), date unknown, and *The Princess de Broglie in Indo-Mogul Costume* (right), 1912. Domain of Chaumont-sur-Loire.
FACING PAGE Carolus-Duran, *Princess Henri-Amédée de Broglie*, oil on canvas, 1884. Domain of Chaumont-sur-Loire.

THE GREAT SALON

The Great Salon, which has extensive views of the Loire, is one of the warmest rooms in the château, with its mural decoration of yellow brocatelle with floral motifs. The furniture, an ensemble that was recently reassembled, recreates the very distinctive art of living enjoyed by wealthy circles in the late nineteenth century. The accumulation of armchairs and refined objects, the presence of tea services, of a samovar, of musical instruments such as the piano and harp, the gambling tables, etc., all bestow on this salon a lived-in, Proustian atmosphere.

FACING PAGE AND PAGES 68–69 The décor of the Great Salon was created in the nineteenth century and completed by the Prince and Princess de Broglie after they acquired the château. The yellow brocatelle decorating the walls was rewoven in 2007, recreating the fabric of the de Broglies' day.
RIGHT Vase with the likeness of Anne of Brittany, Sèvres porcelain, nineteenth century. On permanent loan from the Mobilier National.

THE NINI MEDALLIONS

The château at Chaumont-sur-Loire boasts the world's biggest collection of medallions by Giovanni Battista Nini (1717–1786).

Born in Urbino, Nini started engraving landscapes and portraits at an early age. After a period in Spain, where he went to direct a crystal works near Madrid, he moved to Paris in 1758.

Working both from engravings and from life, the artist made molded medallion portraits in terracotta. These "miniature sculptures" are what made Nini famous, such are the delicacy of the features and the resemblance to the model.

Jacques-Donatien Le Ray de Chaumont, the owner of the château at the time, heard about the artist's reputation and invited him to come and direct its workshops in 1772. Today, we know nothing of Nini's glass production, which has been scattered and lost, but there are some one hundred identified terracotta models, of which sixty-nine are kept at Chaumont-sur-Loire.

These medallions represent important figures of the day such as Louis XV, Louis XVI and Marie-Antoinette, Maria Theresa of Austria, Catherine of Russia, Voltaire, and Benjamin Franklin.

Although the artist made his molds using wax models, he finished the details of his pieces on the still-soft clay before it was fired. This made each casting unique and ensured the high quality of each duplication, since it was retouched by the artist's hand.

FACING PAGE AND ABOVE Giovanni Battista Nini, terracotta medallions depicting, left to right, Louis XV, Louis XVI, Marie-Antoinette, and Benjamin Franklin.

THE MAHARAJA JAGATJIT SINGH OF KAPURTHALA

Visits by the Maharaja Jagatjit Singh of Kapurthala (1872–1949)—who also received the prince and princess at his palace in India—were the occasion for lavish festivities featuring extraordinary illuminations that lit up the château, and sumptuous meals, sometimes concocted by the Indian prince's own chefs. For he brought with him numerous servants, their clothes shimmering with gold and precious stones, some wearing spectacular turbans adorned with glittering plumes. Those present described an atmosphere from the *Thousand and One Nights*, with succulent dishes of lamb curry and rice with silver flakes in the sauce, and magical *pièces montées* representing processions of Hindu princes mounted on elephants caparisoned with gold.

MISS PUNDGI

Offered to the princess by the maharaja, the elephant answering to the name of Miss Pundgi arrived with her first driver in fall 1898 and was housed close to the horses in the stables. She took part in festivities and in hunts with horses and hounds, when she would retrieve with her trunk the game lost in thickets. This exotic guest stayed at the château until 1906, living out the rest of her life in the Jardin d'Acclimatation in Paris.

FACING PAGE Unidentified photographer, *The Maharaja of Kapurthala*, date unknown. Domain of Chaumont-sur-Loire.
ABOVE Unidentified photographer, *The Elephant Miss Pundji in the courtyard of Chaumont-sur-Loire*, early twentieth century. Domain of Chaumont-sur-Loire.
PAGES 74–75 The room for distinguished guests. Stained-glass windows and decoration of the ceiling.

THE GRISAILLES

The grisailles displayed at Chaumont-sur-Loire were added to the windows by the master glassmaker Georges Bardon, who worked on the stained-glass windows for the Dining Room and the three staircases from 1884 to 1895. He also intervened in the chapel and throughout the so-called historic apartments: the Catherine de' Medici Room, the Council Chamber, the Guard Room, and the King's Room.

With great delicacy, he inserted into his new pieces of stained glass the old medallions in grisaille and silver stain, which are also known as rondels.

These grisailles from the fifteenth and sixteenth centuries, obtained by adding metal oxides before firing, were acquired by the Prince de Broglie in Germany.

The rondels giving onto the main courtyard from the Dining Room illustrate four episodes in the life of Solomon: *The Baptism of Solomon, The Building of the Temple of Jerusalem, The Adoration of the Golden Calf,* and *The Queen of Sheba Visits Solomon.*

ABOVE AND FACING PAGE Grisailles illustrating the life of Solomon (from left to right): *The Baptism of Solomon, The Building of the Temple of Jerusalem, The Adoration of the Golden Calf,* and *The Queen of Sheba Visits Solomon.*

THE STABLES

The stables at Chaumont-sur-Loire, built to house some fifty horses, were designed by the architect Paul-Ernest Sanson (1836–1918), who was entrusted with the project by the Prince de Broglie in 1877. The prince wanted them to be the finest in all Europe. Hence the construction of these two luxurious stables—one for the owners of the château, and the other for guests taking part in the prince and princess's mounted hunts. The elegant slate roofs echo those of the château itself, just as the frieze repeats the initials on its façades. Inside, the layout of the Great Stable is the same as when the stables were built. The sizeable collection of harnesses, whips, and steel accessories, some of which were made by the house of Hermès, is considered one of the finest saddleries in Europe. Sanson fitted the stables with arc lamps: in France at the time, only the Opéra Garnier and the Hôtel de Ville in Paris had this kind of electric lighting.

The Great Stable is divided into several parts: the stalls for draft horses, the boxes for thoroughbreds, the stable for ponies, and the stalls for guests' horses. The highly elegant interior layout has remained intact, complete with stalls, cartouches bearing the names of the horses, mangers, drinking troughs in enameled cast iron, and brass balls and hooks.

For the manège, where horses could be put through their paces, or led, the architect made use of the structure of the pottery oven that was part of the manufacture created by Jacques-Donatien Le Ray de Chaumont in the eighteenth century. In the shed for horse-drawn vehicles there are four magnificent models that once belonged to the Prince and Princess de Broglie: a "petit-duc," a "vis-à-vis," a landau, and an omnibus. The stables also house a remarkable gala berlin carriage lined with blue silk, which was made by Ehrler for Prince Nicolas Orlov (1827–1885).

PAGES 78–79 Exterior view of the manège built by Paul-Ernest Sanson during the work in 1877.
FACING PAGE The draft-horses' stable.
RIGHT Today, the stables are home to several works of art, including *Petite Loire* by Mathieu Lehanneur (foreground), *En plein midi* by Klaus Pinter (left), and *Spirale végétale* by Patrick Blanc (background).

FACING PAGE Inside the coach made for Prince Nicolas Orlov.
ABOVE Detail of tassels adorning a carriage.

ABOVE AND FACING PAGE The gala saddlery,
considered one of the finest in France.
PAGES 86–87 View of the château farmyard.

A
KALEIDOSCOPE
OF
GARDENS

INTRODUCTION

The Domain of Chaumont-sur-Loire is a highly original place because it demonstrates all the dimensions, all the facets, and all the temporalities of a garden. First of all, the château is set in a remarkable landscape in Touraine, known as the "Garden of France," an area where the kings of France built residences during the Renaissance, attracted by the perfection of the landscapes and the mildness of the climate in the Loire Valley.

Later, it acquired a huge, English-style park—the historic park laid out in the late nineteenth century by one of the greatest landscape gardeners of the day. Since 2012, it has also boasted a new park, the Prés du Goualoup, whose more natural, wilder atmosphere transports visitors into a radically different world.

The château is also home to the International Garden Festival, with its host of micro-gardens, micro-landscapes, and ephemeral gardens, all concentrated plots of extraordinary invention, where the imagination and talent of gardeners from all over the world are given free rein every year to work with new green scenarios, new plants, new materials, and new ways of thinking about and experiencing gardens. Between these parcels dedicated to the festival, the last few years have seen interstitial gardens grow up, places of permanent invention and research into color and the diversity of foliage and flowers. Since 2012, the Domain has also possessed more permanent contemporary gardens, reflecting the great gardening civilizations, for it was important that all the different periods of the garden should be represented here.

Over recent years, an experimental kitchen garden has been developed, drawing on a mix of new and traditional cultivating techniques that preserve the environment in a harmonious mix of the aesthetic and the useful, the decorative and the nourishing. Here, too, this ecological and pedagogical dimension was necessary to affirm the site's commitment to the cause of environmental preservation.

The seasons follow on here in an extraordinary symphony of colors: spring with its thousands of white bulbs, meadows of great camas, and its blue irises; summer with the sages, the delphiniums, the dahlias, and the thousands of grasses in dominant hues of pink and mauve.

Nor are autumn and winter inactive. From September there are asters and Indian lilacs, then October brings the richly colored leaves of the alleys of trees. Later come the luxuriant winter gardens, protected from the harsh cold in glasshouses.

Ephemeral and perennial gardens, a historical park and a contemporary park—different worlds, all perpetually evolving, never alike from one day to another, from one hour to the next: such is the infinitely diverse world of the gardens at Chaumont-sur-Loire.

FACING PAGE Ulli Heckmann, "La Possibilité d'une île" (Possibility of an Island), 2018.

ALL HISTORICAL GARDEN PERIODS

Although it is best known for its international festivals, with its annually renewed palette of gardens, the Domain of Chaumont-sur-Loire is not only a place for the creation of ephemeral gardens: it is also home to the different historical eras of garden design.

The era of the historic park created by Henri Duchêne in the nineteenth century, on older foundations; the era of the twenty-five-acre park conceived by Louis Benech in 2012; and the era of the gardens in the Prés du Goualoup, reflecting the great gardening civilizations, constitute a temporal grounding and an essential framework for the artistic experiments carried out on the estate. At Chaumont-sur-Loire, some gardens—those of the festival—live for only a season, while the parks and other gardens belong in a period of time and enjoy a longevity that are radically different. More than seven hundred gardens have been created here since the inception of the festival, and it is for this continual movement that the site is famous; this is what makes it a laboratory and observatory of gardening trends.

ABOVE The Chinese garden, created in collaboration with the Museum of Chinese Gardens and Landscape Architecture in Beijing.
FACING PAGE The "Hualu, Ermitage sur Loire" garden by Che Bing Chiu.

THE PARKS

THE HISTORIC PARK

The historic park that today can be observed around the château was created between 1884 and 1887 by the great landscape architect Henri Duchêne, at the request of Prince Henri-Amédée de Broglie and his wife, Marie-Charlotte-Constance Say. To do so, they began by transferring to the village the church standing on the slopes, together with some hundred houses, which the new owners felt were too close to their residence. The cemetery and kitchen garden were also pushed back to allow the creation of a magnificent English-style park of forty-two acres. This historic park did not start from scratch: it had inherited from the eighteenth century a central walk on the southeastern side, planted with chestnut trees, as well as an avenue of linden trees abutting the eastern flank of the château, and the sumptuous cedars planted by the Count d'Aramon, owner of Chaumont from 1830 to 1847.

Hence the creation of the big circular pathway, the elliptical paths, the extensive lawns, and clumps of trees, setting up a harmonious overall atmosphere and providing a superb setting for the château. The great landscape gardener succeeded in creating a homogenous whole, combining views of the Loire with splendid green vistas.

In order to allow visitors to cross the ravine that he created on the other side of the ramp leading to the château, in 1884 Duchêne designed a metal footbridge totally covered with cement fashioned to imitate wood, an extraordinarily rustic-looking structure. He even created a picturesque hollow tree trunk to hide the staircase linking the two levels of the bridge.

FACING PAGE The historic park created by Henri Duchêne in the nineteenth century is punctuated by giant clumps of trees inherited from the eighteenth century or introduced by later owners.

LEFT The footbridge created by Henri Duchêne in 1884.
PAGES 98-99 The landscape gardener created
a harmonious ensemble extending over forty-two
acres and offering visitors a perfect mix of green
lawns, copses, and paths for walking.

RIGHT *L'Œil de l'oubli* (The Eye of Forgetfulness), created by Anne and Patrick Poirier in 2010, stands in the ice store.

THE ICE STORE

Ice stores were an essential feature of châteaux whose owners frequently held receptions. At Chaumont-sur-Loire, this store kept drinks cool and helped to conserve particular foods, making an important contribution to the quality of the welcome extended to the prestigious guests of the Prince and Princess de Broglie. Lined with stones, this conical pit is ideally positioned at the top of a ravine now known as the Vallon des Brumes (Valley of Mists). It is seven and a half yards deep and just under ten yards across. Today, its sides are covered with ivy and moss, but in the past there was a stone stairway leading to the bottom. This store, located not far from the kitchens, could hold tons of ice, which were protected by a covering of plants that made it possible to keep the blocks stored in the stone for a very long time. Today, the ice store houses a sculpture by Anne and Patrick Poirier: *L'Œil de l'oubli* (The Eye of Forgetfulness).

PRÉS DU GOUALOUP PARK

Created by the landscape designer Louis Benech, who also restored the historic park by felling a number of trees and planting new ones, Prés du Goualoup Park, which stands on land left unattended since the time of the de Broglies, was primarily designed to provide a fitting space for welcoming visitors to the festival, the growing popularity of which made an extension to the garden a real necessity.

This twenty-five-acre park, conceived and inaugurated in 2012, had been neglected for many years and yet there were still visible traces of the old park laid out by Duchêne. Since the number of visitors had grown considerably, there was a need to offer them new spaces where they could stroll and muse at peace. Another part of Louis Benech's commission was to conceive new plots that would later contain the gardens inspired by the great gardening traditions. All of this motivated the celebrated landscape designer, whose work is renowned for its subtlety, to create a large circular path, echoing the pathways laid out by Duchêne in the historic park, and to construct vistas giving onto the château.

Clearing away the old copses, and particularly the cedars and the plane trees, while keeping the hawthorn hedges, Louis Benech planted new trees of the same kind and centered his composition on a big central meadow that, in springtime, becomes a sea of daisies and buttercups—these flowers miraculously re-flowered after completion of the landscaping work. Paths were laid out through this wilder space, enabling visitors to go from one grove to another. The plots set aside for the future gardens were located on the edge of the main path, leaving the big central meadow free.

FACING PAGE Irises and ornamental garlic,
Prés du Goualoup park.
PAGES 104–05 "Le Jardin Miroir" (The Mirror Garden)
in Prés du Goualoup park, created in 2014
by the Domain's gardeners.

THE INTERNATIONAL
GARDEN FESTIVAL

AN INTERNATIONALLY RENOWNED ADVENTURE

The International Garden Festival of Chaumont-sur-Loire, an event that has acquired a global reputation, is original in more ways than one. In contrast to many other horticultural events, this is a festival of ephemeral gardens that last only six months. These gardens are real creative works, conceived and made by multidisciplinary, international teams. This makes the festival a kind of laboratory, where new trends can be introduced and disseminated.

The International Garden Festival in Chaumont-sur-Loire was created in 1992, at a time when there was a massive revival of interest in gardens following a long period postwar in which gardens had been neglected in favor of replacing destroyed buildings.

In 1980s France, over 80 percent of the population lived in cities or suburbs. The countryside had lost much of its population and the urban landscape had changed considerably. Air pollution and nostalgia for a certain quality of life closer to nature now played an important role in stimulating the new desire to get "back to the garden" to quote Joni Mitchell in "Woodstock." At the same time, new landscape designers, who were veritable artists, were emerging all around the world, their creations boldly breaking with the traditional vision of the garden. This conjunction is the reason why the art of gardens has continued to grow in popularity over the last thirty years.

The International Garden Festival was the brainchild of an enthusiastic ideas man, Jean-Paul Pigeat. He worked at the Pompidou Center in Paris, and became adviser to Minister of Culture Jack Lang in his policy for renovating national gardens and landscapes. One of Pigeat's ideas was to create a garden on the roof of the Pompidou Center itself. That did not happen, but it was thanks to him, and to the support of the minister, who was also the mayor of nearby Blois, that Chaumont-sur-Loire became an extraordinary event for experimentation in the field of landscape and gardens.

Having identified the valley and meadow where the festival could be held—and in that joyous euphoria that marks the build-up to such events—the design of the plots that would host the ephemeral gardens was entrusted to the great Belgian landscape designer Jacques Wirtz. His design referred to the form of the tulip tree leaves characteristic of the gardens at Chaumont. Indeed, the designs of the twenty-six experimental gardens, each with an area of three hundred square yards, take the form of a branch of *Liriodendron tulipifera* or Virginia tulip tree.

With over seven hundred projects carried out since it began, the festival at Chaumont-sur-Loire has profoundly changed the way we look at gardens and done much to modernize their image. A platform where practitioners of highly diverse disciplines can experiment, Chaumont-sur-Loire remains a space of permanent invention that can claim to have introduced new plant forms and techniques for the first time. Here, joyously juxtaposing the most conceptual works with more popular expressions of the art of the garden, this cocktail of sometimes surprising styles is what makes the event so appealing and inventive.

Every year, the International Garden Festival of Chaumont-sur-Loire continues to play its role as pathfinder, revealing new trends and new talents. The gardens are at once diverse and different, often utterly at odds with classical rules, sometimes closer to artistic installations than to the traditional world of horticulture, and sometimes very close to nature.

At Chaumont-sur-Loire, design, art, and architecture all have their place in the garden. Structures, textures, and colors are used in ways that are both surprising and innovative, and sometimes even provocative. And yet every year these gardens, which bend the rules

FACING PAGE Xavier Bonnaud, Stéphane Berthier, Clément Boucher, Fabien Gantoin, Étienne Panien, Olivier Duraysseix, and Guillaume Pezet, "Les Bulbes fertiles" (The Fertile Bulbs), 2011.

and twist forms, attract ever-growing numbers of visitors and professionals. Several trends are in evidence in the art of the garden today: the themes at the Chaumont festival and the answers it provides both reveal and reflect these tendencies. The International Garden Festival highlights the fact that the contemporary garden is no more isolated from the great changes afoot in our society than are any other arts. Rather, the garden faithfully echoes them. A number of resonant sociological and environmental realities we are now witnessing are having an obvious impact on our relation to gardens and are helping to spur new approaches to this art. Awareness of ecological issues, for example, is resulting in new attitudes, with greater respect for natural resources. Climate change has clearly had an impact on the way we think about gardens.

Parallel to this acute concern with the state of our planet is another of the big trends in contemporary gardens: a shift toward solidarity, with a rise in the number of shared gardens, workers' gardens, and community gardens. This tendency is related to economic issues, concerns about food supply, an interest in growing one's own vegetables, and the desire to share one's time and garden with others. The rise in therapeutic gardens, also a strong trend, is part of the same movement.

But it is above all the creative angle that has driven the tremendous rise of the art of gardening in recent years. Conceptual gardens, philosophical gardens, and artistic gardens are endlessly surprising, with their innovative materials and their creative ways of using traditional materials, including growing new vegetables or devising new ways of combining and using them, not to mention many other ingenious and bold techniques.

At the crossroads of these major trends in contemporary gardening, and attentive to those essential issues facing our society, the International Garden Festival hosts some one hundred and fifty garden designers every year, of all ages and geographical origins. Each year, an international competition is organized. Numerous teams around the world work on the set theme, the choice of which is itself quite a challenge, because it must be both in sync with current preoccupations and touch on deeper questions.

Every year, the jury at the Domain, made up of passionate experts on art and gardens, assesses three hundred projects. Out of these, it selects twenty-five. Every year, the jury is chaired by a different figure in order to ensure a new and original vision of the special world of gardens. Over the years, among those who have agreed to take part in the very particular adventure that is a new festival are baroque conductor William Christie, neurologist Jean-Pierre Changeux, botanist Jean-Marie Pelt, landscape designer Louis Benech, historian and color specialist Michel Pastoureau, collector and garden lover Maryvonne Pinault, chef Alain Passard, novelist Jean Echenoz, television cultural presenter Bernard Pivot, and film director Coline Serreau.

FACING PAGE Timothée Blancpain and Philippe Caillaud, "Metempsychosis" garden, 2010.
PAGES 110–11 George Richardson and Jules Arthur, "Bon thé bon genre" (Posh Tea, Posh People), 2010.

THE POWER OF MULTIDISCIPLINARITY

One of the unique features of the International Garden Festival is the multidisciplinary nature of the teams that design and create the gardens. For these are not gardens created exclusively or even mainly by landscape designers. Most of the time, these designers team up with architects, designers, stage designers, and artists, and it is this particular alliance of talents and visions that helps to keep the idea of the garden constantly on the move. An architect will not look at space in the same way as a landscape designer, who will think of the development of the plants and the permanent transformation of the scenery and garden, whereas someone who works in the theater or cinema will have yet another idea of visual presentation.

At Chaumont-sur-Loire, artistic disciplines complement each other, influence each other, and give rise to innovations, to crossovers that strengthen the festival's experimental side. Sometimes, it is non-specialists from outside the world of landscaping who create the most beautiful gardens.

FACING PAGE AND ABOVE Leon Kluge, "Cuisine africaine" (African Cuisine) garden, 2015.
PAGES 114–15 Romain Bardin, Manon Chevalier, and Antonietta Masillo, "Le Jardin déchêné" (The Garden Unoaked), 2014.

ABOVE AND FACING PAGE Carine Balayn, Dorian Dietschy,
Chloé Martin, and Éric Sartre, "Le Jardin du teinturier"
(The Dyer's Garden), 2015.

THE EPHEMERAL GARDENS

Before considering the innovations, inventions, and ideas fostered by the International Garden Festival, a brief overview of the main themes of the last ten years will help convey the festival's distinctive and immediately recognizable atmosphere, as recorded by the camera of Eric Sander—whose sensitivity is remarkably attuned to seeing and capturing the creativity, imagination, and poetry of the gardens at Chaumont- sur-Loire.

Environmental questions, which are close to my heart, were strongly present in recent festival themes. The main objective of the 2011 festival, "Gardens of the Future or the Art of Happy Biodiversity," was to urge rebellion against a certain form of horticultural standardization and to raise awareness of the extinction of several species. This celebration of the diversity "that gives us the pleasure of discovery, the beauty of landscapes, the meeting of languages, and the richness of exchanges" was central to the theme. "[B]oth a source and an end in itself, the expression of nature in its original form, of transformation and organization, of utility and pleasure," the garden "brings together all the richness of the world, everything nature gives us, and all that knowledge and history have brought in terms of transformations, organization and rites, creativity, and expression. The garden is a celebration of the diversity of people and nature, of living species, of their coexistence and of the necessary balance between them." ("Gardens of the Future or the Art of Happy Biodiversity" program, 2011.) Today, this equilibrium is under threat, for we have drawn on our natural resources as if they were a bottomless well, with no concern either for their preservation or their uniqueness. The accelerated extinction of living species is jeopardizing biodiversity and the diversity of nature's life forces.

Beyond simple matters of botany and plants, a garden tends to become a little ecosystem, a place where flowers, plants, herbs, seeds, and fauna are able to come together and magnify their differences, living together in a profusion that blends both the time of their origin and the time of invention, wilderness, and transformation. To demonstrate this infinite richness, this abundance, to highlight its virtues and potential and the fruitful accidents of extreme diversity, encouraging the public to respect and celebrate nature: such was the objective of the 2011 festival. The idea was that, while gardens cannot save the world all on their own, they can offer more opportunities for this biodiversity, take it in new directions, to other receptive places, and spread botanical knowledge. To name plants and seeds, to think about how they should be conserved, is already to grant them an existence.

At the 2011 International Garden Festival visitors could see and explore gardens that acted as a warning, and attend workshops on diversity. While keeping all their magic, their beauty, and their aesthetic power, these gardens exalted biodiversity and re-enchanted the world. For example, the "Garden of Lost Plants" took visitors into a strange cemetery, an accumulation of hundreds of labels bearing the names of extinct plants and species, palpably conveying the negative development of biodiversity. One of the emblematic gardens in that year's festival (and which, since then, has gone international), was the "Sculptillonnage" garden which, in order to encourage composting, presented extraordinary mushrooms sculpted from meshed materials, called "champicomposteurs," and which contained an accumulation of seasonal vegetable debris. "The Transparency of the Worm" garden invited visitors underground, where they could witness the scale of underground life and gauge the major role played by earthworms, which recycle waste by digesting the debris of plants and organic matter.

The 2016 International Garden Festival, "Gardens from the Coming Century," was also inspired by ecological concerns. Participants were encouraged to come up with solutions for our green environment. It is clear that ecological research and scientific and technical

FACING PAGE Frédérique Larinier, Gaël Bardon, and Emmanuel Puybonnieux, "Que vienne la pluie" (Let It Rain), 2016.

RIGHT Lélia Demoisy, Julie Mahieu, Adèle Hopquin, and Maud Negron, "Je reste" (I Remain), 2016.

investigations of all kinds are observing, fertilizing, and reinventing this ever-changing world. Permaculture, transgenesis, biocontrol, aquaponics, hydroponics, green chemistry, phytore-mediation, vertical farms, synergistic vegetable plots—these are just some of the facets of this amazing adventure of the living world, in which experimentation, prospecting, and dis-covery combine tradition, ecology, and technological progress, yet without losing sight of the human dimension or of poetic imagination.

Whether tied up with the adventure of "incredible edibles," "intelligent seeds," spec-tacular multi-grafted fruit trees, or with the chlorophyllic fluorescence of plants, mod-ern-day gardens have a thousand-and-one ways of astonishing us. The aim was to present gardens that address the great questions of our time, such as climate change, rising sea levels, "floating gardens," and the link between habitat and gardens. The mes-sage of the "Je reste" (I Remain) garden, which evoked the problem of rising sea levels caused by global warming, was brought home dramatically by the spectacular floods that occurred all around France in 2016. Visitors came upon a house sunk in water, with only its roof visible. They were confronted with the ways in which populations would have to adapt to such conditions. Indeed, while the gardens in the 2016 festival denounced the often disastrous consequences of climate change, they also offered solutions, and in particular crops and forms of agriculture adapted to this new situation. "Que vienne la pluie" (Let It Rain), for example, presented a poetic world of delicate gardens floating on the water, supported by living willow, like the water cultures of Inle Lake in Burma. Other landscapers presented vertical gardens, like those of "Néo-Noé" (Neo-Noah). Using plants as supports, working as filters to depollute the water and feed plants, this garden demonstrated that the techniques of phyto-purification and aquaponics, which preserve nature, could quite easily be put into practice in today's gardens, let alone tomorrow's. These techniques were also central to the poetical "Jardin flottant du songe" (Floating Garden of Dreams).

Other gardens in 2016 were edible, as could be seen when visiting the "Jardin qui se savoure" (Garden to Relish) and "Forêt alimentaire" (Food Forest), and yet others regen-erated themselves after a disaster, as in the "Phœnix" of the 2017 festival. There have been dry gardens, able to withstand a lack of water, as in the magnificent "Jardin des émer-gences" (Garden of Emergences) of 2016, which showcased the energy and remarkable resourcefulness of plants with a superb display of yuccas and other Mediterranean plants capable of enduring long dry spells. Even when the gardens are conceptual or philosoph-ical, a garden festival cannot allow itself to forget botanical concerns. That is why festival themes such as "Extraordinary Gardens, Collectors' Gardens" (2015) and "Flower Power" had the great virtue of drawing public attention to the infinite riches of plant life.

FACING PAGE Jean-Philippe Poirée-Ville and Gérard Pontet, "Le Jardin flottant du songe" (Floating Garden of Dreams), 2016.
PAGES 124–25 Corinne Julhiet-Détroyat and Claude Pasquer, "Sculptillonnage", 2011.

"EXTRAORDINARY GARDENS, COLLECTORS' GARDENS"

The aim of the International Garden Festival of Chaumont-sur-Loire in 2015, "Extraordinary Gardens, Collectors' Gardens," was to showcase our plant heritage and the need for real diversity of plant life, which is so often damaged by excessive standardization. A number of nurserymen and women have indeed dedicated their lives—and often it is quite a struggle—to protecting, safeguarding, and developing remarkable collections of plants that are threatened with extinction by the simplifying tendencies and rules of the market. Driven by the same passion as art collectors, they collect, preserve, and multiply rare and original plant varieties. They also share a taste for research and the excitement of discovering unique specimens, sometimes from the other end of the world. In terms of gardens, we are indebted to these specialists for maintaining endangered plant biodiversity.

The 2015 festival therefore presented extraordinary gardens, which played on the accumulation of rare and exceptional plants, displayed in a most unusual way, almost as though the gardens were museums. The creations on offer that year were utterly novel, well off the beaten track, featuring unexpected plants and flowers that no one would have expected to find.

For example, a garden going by the evocative name of "Carnivore Parc" displayed an extraordinary collection of Droseras and Sarracenias, among others, which are seriously endangered by the uniformization of production. The biggest French collection of carnivorous plants recently disappeared in favor of industrial productions, seriously reducing the range of possibilities.

In the "Porte-bonheur" (Lucky Charm) garden, an exceptional collection of clover with highly unusual forms and colors showed the public the remarkable diversity of these plants, which remain little known and are unjustly despised.

The "Jardin des graines" (Seeds Garden), presented by the association of botanical gardens in France and French-speaking countries showed, in the middle of a giant sieve used for sorting them, the infinite diversity and importance of seeds. Their aesthetic beauty was in evidence, as was their rich fertility: a limitless resource—on condition that humankind respects and preserves these treasures.

In "Silence ! Ça mousse" (Silence! It Foams), a sublime moss garden demonstrated both the value and multiplicity of species of bryophytes, which are little known by the general public.

In "Le Collectionneur de l'ombre" (The Shadow Collector), nearly two hundred kinds of fern, out of the one thousand four hundred varieties that exist on our planet, were exhibited on metal shelves and in crates, giving the strange and fascinating impression of having been left on the tarmac at an airport.

Particularly eye-catching were the presentations that came close to the world of art. For example, there was a spectacular composition of blue plants in the "Nuances" garden, a museum-like display featuring a collection of rare palm trees, and again a genuine plant library, or *phytothèque*. And there was a genuine ark—not Noah's but Linnaeus's Ark ("L'Arche de Linné"), in reference to the great Swedish botanist—bringing together plants of all kinds, from every kind of terrain, from humid to desert-like, greeting visitors to that year's festival rich in surprising plants.

ABOVE Oriane Bodin, Laurène Pillot, Clément Villette,
and Laurent Beaubreuil (Agrocampus Ouest, Angers),
"L'Arche de Linné" (Linnaeus's Ark), 2015.
RIGHT Claire Dugard and Christelle David,
"Porte-bonheur" (Lucky Charm), 2015.
PAGES 130–31 Pierre Labat and Delphine Guéret,
"Nuances," 2015.

"FLOWER POWER"

As for the 2017 festival, its purpose was to celebrate the power of flowers, whether in a direct reference to the 1960s and 1970s, when flowers were a symbol of peace in troubled times, or to the timeless power of all things floral.

In all ages and on every continent, art and literature have always praised the importance and incomparable beauty of flowers. Their graphic perfection and infinite diversity has inspired endless praise, while the seductive, heady charm of their scent and the delicacy of their colors bewitch, as is well known, both our senses and our souls. Fugacious, fragile, and powerful all at the same time, flowers are endlessly amazing, troubling, charming, and therapeutic. What remains of that power today? Is it still pertinent, in the world of landscape and gardens? How is this bewitching power of flowers being showcased and enhanced? This is the question that competitors for that year's festival had to answer.

The objective was to encourage the emergence of innovative, contemporary stagings and novel combinations of flowers and their settings, all designed to inspire the visitor to dream.

For example, "Le Pouvoir des sorcières" (The Power of Witches) celebrated the virtues of well-known medicinal plants associated with those mysterious and feared mediators between man and nature that are witches, all in a garden which featured ominous accents of black and dark red. Visitors also came upon a "Fleur du mal" (Flower of Evil) garden in an abandoned village, which was home to a lost people of opium eaters, full of forbidden and notorious plants known for their powerful hallucinogenic effects. Irresistibly perfumed flowers could be savored in "Apis vertigo," where one could see sublime and rebellious blooms escaping from the chests in which "The Man Who Loved Flowers" had locked them up.

The garden is also the place par excellence for the expression of sensuality, joy, and synesthesia. It is therefore not surprising to see that the themes chosen include the seven deadly sins and gardens of delirium and earthly delights.

FACING PAGE Sung Hye Park and Byung-Eun Min de Gaulejac, "Le Pouvoir des sorcières" (The Power of Witches), 2017. PAGES 134–35 Jeanne Martin, Coralie Michel, Julien Magnan, Franck Masanell, and Guillaume Nouvellon (Agrocampus Ouest, Angers), "L'homme qui aimait les fleurs" (The Man Who Loved Flowers), 2017.

"GARDENS OF THE DEADLY SINS"

The 2014 festival addressed the question of the deadly sins, starting from the premise that the garden can be a place of unfettered hedonism and unimpeded freedom.

A singular space, a "magical place which, to blossom, relies on the rule that subversion is possible and which, to thrive, knows where its limits lie," the idea of the garden conjured up at Chaumont-sur-Loire in 2014 was a "heady expression of the deadly sins," ("Gardens of the Deadly Sins" program, 2014) between excess and moderation, restraint and abandon. In their distinctive ways, these gardens celebrated greed, pride, idleness, and sensuality. They also evoked anger and envy.

Bold perfumes, sinful and stupefying plants, plots with unexpected atmospheres, suggesting delicious sins, welcomed visitors who were surprised and charmed by the fantasies and excess of all kinds, subtlety translated into the language of flowers.

So it was that visitors went from the evocation of avarice in the accumulation of a gilded treasure in "Ma cassette" (My Chest), the garden of Molière's miser, Harpagon, to the fantasies of luxury cherished by a skinflint gardener in a garden, with two contrasting facets, titled "Quand l'avare rêve" (When the Miser Dreams).

Greed found its place, with "Gourmanderie" (Gluttony), while the "Haute culture" (High Culture) and "Le Domaine de Narcisse" (The Domain of Narcissus) gardens presented derivations of pride. The only option was to take refuge in the "Jardin des pécheresses" (Sinners' Garden) where a confessional offered visitors the chance to be forgiven all their failings in a plot overgrown with plants linked to the different sins: pride, envy, anger, idleness, lust, avarice, and greed.

FACING PAGE Camille Luquet, Caroline Leroux, and Céline Klipfel, "Ma Cassette" (My Chest), 2014.
PAGES 138–39 Carlotta Montefoschi, Niccolo Cau, Luigi Rebecchini, Francesco Jacques Dias, Ricardo Walker Campos, Francesca Romana Guanaschelli, and Maria Cecilia Villanis Ziani, "Le Domaine de Narcisse" (The Domain of Narcissus), 2014.

"GARDENS OF SENSATIONS"

But another year, in 2013, it was the delights engendered by the senses that were explored by the gardens at Chaumont-sur-Loire, where the theme was "Gardens of Sensations."

"A mini-version of the world, the garden is there for walking, feeling, listening, tasting, seeing, and touching; the air comes and goes with the wind, light and shadow interplay, the cold and heat, smooth and rough, liquid and solid, flat and sloping, movement and lolling, shouts and whispers tumble one after the other in unison with the senses and sensations. The body rejoices in a kinaesthesia reminiscent of a physical and spiritual experience of the world." ("Gardens of Sensations" program, 2013.) Such was the fundamental sensuality that this year's theme set out to showcase. This of course meant evoking Baudelairean "synesthesias," but also immersing visitors in an extraordinary universe that stunned them with its superabundance of diverse and concomitant sensations.

The celebration of sensations can enable us as city dwellers to refresh our sense of self, forgetting the glass and stone and virtual worlds that alienate us from nature's harmony. Here, the repressed senses were bewitched in a garden whose fragrance, materials, and sounds mixed deliciously to captivate the soul. Extraordinary flowers exuded the perfume of spices and offered a taste of sugar, honey, or vanilla. And there were also surprising leaves that had the taste of strawberry or chocolate, the softness of feathers or velvet. Aromas, flavors, and fragrances mixed to felicitous effect in a surprising and fecund euphoria.

This year offered, for example, an immersive experience at the heart of an astonishing "Jardin à frôler" (Garden to Brush Against), where visitors themselves composed a sublime and singular musical work in dialogue with nature, simply by passing close to the tactile fibers—creepers hung from a sculpture-tree. They could also hear the messages murmured by the trees in a poetic "Jardin d'amour" (Garden of Love).

They could sit at the foot of old-fashioned-looking "Meules impressionnantes" (Impressionist/Impressive Haystacks), which were perfumed by the smell of hay and looked as if they came straight out of an impressionist painting. They could breathe in heady perfumes when they put their heads in helmets called *sniffettes*.

They could enjoy a synesthetic experience combining all types of sensations in the garden called "Voir les sons, entendre les couleurs" (See Sounds, Hear colors).

In 2012, the twenty-first International Garden Festival took us down a merrily mad trail with its theme, "Gardens of Delight, Gardens of Delirium."

FACING PAGE Emma Boutot and Olivier Simon,
"Les Parfums du vignoble" (Scents of the Vineyard), 2013.
PAGES 142–43 Robin Godde, "Des meules impressionnantes"
(Impressionist/Impressive Haystacks), 2013.

"GARDENS OF DELIGHT, GARDENS OF DELIRIUM"

An epitome of harmony, symbolically linked to the idyllic scenery of Arcadia, the garden is often considered a place of ultimate bliss.

In reference to this tradition, the gardens of the 2012 festival were designed to be, ideally, gardens of delight. But, given their touch of folly, they also had to be places of unbridled imagination, botanical luxuriance, and extravagant stagings. Deliberately audacious, they were expected to engender surprise, wonder, and even a sense of the fantastical.

The 2012 festival thus offered surprises of all kinds, confronting us with veritable cabinets of curiosities, behind which were real technical performances in terms of aural, visual, hydraulic, and olfactory effects.

Whether they presented extraordinary topiary, contemporary creations and follies, eccentric plants, or phenomenal fruits and vegetables, the gardens seen in 2012 took us through the looking glass, into fabulous and unreal worlds.

That year, "Le Jardin bleu d'Absolem" (Absolem's Blue Garden) did indeed transport visitors into the exuberant and hallucinatory world of Lewis Carroll, down a metaphorical rabbit hole, into a smoky forest peopled with gray eucalyptuses, faced with a fantastical flight of blue butterflies.

As for "Coulisse d'un festin" (Behind the Scenes at a Feast), it was like a kitchen garden gone crazy, a veggie heaven, offering a sweet overdose at the heart of its magic plot: crazy artichokes, giant leeks, extraordinary colocynths, and pumpkins neighboring with toothsome melons, oversize little gems, and Chinese lanterns, in an intriguing display of fascinating multicolored jars.

"Paradis terrestre" (Earthly Paradise) led visitors into the heart of a legendary and luxuriant garden adorned with lantern-fruits, extravagant fountains, and fabulous trees, uniting all the pleasures, in never-ending joy.

"En vert" (In Green) presented an inverted, surrealist world where darkly mysterious characters had their heads plunged into the vegetation, as if to listen to the song of the earth, their feet thrusting skywards, resting on ladders that seemed to rise all the way to the heavens.

FACING PAGE Étienne Rivière, Aline Gayou, Mathilde Coineau, Marion Delage, Pauline Bertin, and Laura Yoro, "Coulisses d'un festin" (Behind the Scenes at a Feast), 2012.
PAGES 146–47 Patrice Gobert, Marie-Christine Loriers, Pascal Montel, Béatrice Tollu, Thierry Dalcant, and Olivier Thomas, "En vert" (In Green), 2012.

"GARDENS OF COLOR"

No one can deny that color is an indispensable part of the world of gardens. Plants and flowers are or should be to the landscape designer what gouaches are to the painter. Practitioners of both disciplines seek to bring forth harmonies, contrasts, and equilibriums, and work tirelessly on their chromatic echoes, on effects, creating skeins of radiating color.

For the year of 2009, the International Garden Festival showed that the vegetable palette used by artists and landscape designers could present an infinite variety of associations, whose power and harmony have an undeniable effect on the senses and the mind.

This festival put forward sensuous gardens rich in nuances, whether monochrome or with subtle graduations, or offered up parcels of bright colors. The gardens also celebrated the importance of dye-yielding plants and pigments used throughout the world, and especially by artists.

Intense reds, deep blues, whites, or blacks—this was certainly a year when the gardens at Chaumont surprised us with their poetry. This theme of color effectively gave rise to some very spectacular gardens, like "Voir rouge" (See Red), which offered a hilly landscape planted with surveillance cameras, flashing lights, and uniformly red plants, combined with mulch consisting of purple sawdust. This monochrome color was designed to draw attention to the state of watchfulness or high alert in which we now permanently live.

The "Jardin mange-tête" (Head-Eating Garden) opened up a colorful individual experience by offering visitors the chance to see the world in pink or blue, simply by slipping their heads into a translucent colored bubble.

"Lessive en fleurs" (Laundry Flowers) played on the subtle harmony between a line of washing in pastel colors and beds of blue, pink, and mauve dye-producing plants.

"Recto-verso" opposed two colors: green and red, thanks to a subtle topographical system using slopes and counter-slopes. Visitors entered via a red garden and came out via a green garden. As for "Du noir de l'eau au blanc du ciel" (From Black Waters to White Skies), it was inspired by Escher's garden and offered up enchanting, bi-colored paths, going from black to white, via gray.

The power of plantlife and its soothing effects, and the role of the therapeutic garden, which are increasingly discussed subjects nowadays, were at the heart of the gardens in the 2010 festival.

ABOVE AND RIGHT Patrice Gobert, Marie-Christine Loriers,
Pascal Montel, and Béatrice Tollu, "Voir rouge" (See Red), 2009.
PAGES 152–53 Anouk Vogel and Katarina Brandt, "Du noir de l'eau
au blanc du ciel" (From Black Waters to White Skies), 2009.

"BODY AND SOUL GARDENS"

A garden has a profound effect on our bodies and souls. "A place of wellbeing, of *otium*, as the Ancients called rest, a garden is above all 'the place where you feel good." ("Body and Soul Gardens" program, 2010.) Working on all the senses, it is the place of calm and serenity, conducive to meditation and dream. But one also finds there plants that heal the body, and, more generally, medicinal herbs, and aromatic and condiment plants. The garden, and nature, are the origin of numerous medicines. Sometimes considered as a space for forgetting our cares, a garden is also a place that reconstructs and heals the spirit. "Touching the earth" acts on our inner equilibrium. We know all about "the power of the gardens on cerebral and neurological pathologies." (2010 festival.) Psychic and physical effects were therefore on the agenda in settings designed to foster positive energies. Like another form of resilience, "the garden also cares for injured landscapes, which it embellishes, restores, and repairs; it even contributes to purifying nature when it has been poisoned by human beings [...] with depolluting and detoxifying plants. [...] The garden cares for the soul, but it also arouses passions, 'body and soul' commitments in the cause of beauty, happiness, and well-being." (2010 festival.)

Nobody can be unaware of how the garden takes care of us, and thus helps to take care of and heal those in pain. We know of the benefits of horticultural therapy, phytotherapy, and hedonic therapy. Providing therapy for both the soul and the body, the gardens in 2010 were a veritable invitation into a world of serenity and inner peace.

In the "Hommage à Lady Day" garden, Billie Holiday's commitment to her art, body and soul, was expressed in a garden planted with poppy flowers, in a reference to artificial paradises, in the middle of which stood a magnificent piano with a microphone. The inimitable voice of this legendary jazz singer could be heard among the flowers.

"Ma terre, mater" (My Earth, Mother) took visitors back to the original mother earth, into a cocoon recalling the softness of the womb, planted with sweet and richly perfumed white verbena flowers, where they could sit in deep wicker chairs, conducive to hypnotic immersion in the fragrances and colors.

"Bon thé bon genre" (Posh Tea, Posh People) invited visitors to an English-style tea ceremony amid a luxuriant garden planted with wild lamps and plants for herbal teas, all hidden behind an extraordinary wall of antique porcelain.

"Igloolik ultima" welcomed visitors into an igloo covered with dozens of species of different sages, with eminently therapeutic qualities and perfumes, delicately arrayed in apple-green pots on finely wrought exterior shelves.

The "Main dans la main" (Hand in Hand) garden created by the great choreographer Benjamin Millepied encouraged spectators to take the pink and blue paths marked out on the ground, as in traditional choreography. Men and women became dancers for a day, moving around with grace and rigor in the middle of plants whose colors were carefully chosen.

As for "Rêve de Pantagruel" (Pantagruel's Dream), it presented an extraordinary table on which glasses and cutlery in delicate hues invited visitors to share a remarkable virtual feast of plants. Nature's food is good for the well-being of the soul.

FACING PAGE Benjamin Millepied, "Main dans la main" (Hand in Hand), 2010.
PAGES 156–57 Olivier Hostiou, Marie Forêt, and Laurent Weiss, "Ma terre, mater" (My Earth, Mother), 2010.

LABORATORY AND OBSERVATORY

The International Garden Festival of Chaumont-sur-Loire quickly became a platform for exchange and research, for social and intellectual connection and reflection around the subject of gardens. Every year, it presents what is a veritable trends report, a laboratory for observing the main interests in the universe of gardens, worldwide. It is attracting ever-growing numbers of visitors, both amateurs and professionals, thanks to its characteristic freedom of expression.

At Chaumont-sur-Loire, inventions and games with the elements and with materials and plants have resulted in many innovations, a good number of which had, and still have, international resonance.

Everybody knows, for example, the plant walls of Patrick Blanc, still visible at Chaumont behind the current kitchen garden. Their planetary success story began in 1994, when they were shown in the festival of that year. These living works now form sumptuous and unexpected oases in the heart of cities. The botanist's idea of using the vertical growth of plants, analogous to that of primal forests, was transformed into a spectacular invention, making it possible to create gardens without earth on the walls of polluted metropolises. The plants grow on an underlayer of felt, with a water supply and mineral salts helping to support their development. In 2010 Patrick Blanc conceived a very innovative creation in the stables at Chaumont-sur-Loire, a piece on the border between art and botany. Inventing a new structure—a giant leaf curling around itself until it came to form a secret grotto, open to the sky—the botanist's aim was to develop different biotopes by means of carefully conceived folds that created different types of exposure to the light.

The extraordinary plant arabesques of Jean-Philippe Poirée-Ville constitute another remarkable invention. This multi-talented artist-landscape designer uses sphagnum (peat moss) that is packed with seeds. These develop with stunning luxuriance over the season, drawing fantastical plantlike forms and scripts. His *Sylphes*, giant creepers which dialogued with the château in 2012, and his outgrowth "Jardin flottant du songe" (Floating Garden of Dreams), seen in 2016, captivated visitors.

Structures made from woven branches, both dry and living, are also frequently used by the creators of gardens at Chaumont-sur-Loire. Dry branches have the advantage of creating natural limits or original structures. Living willow branches woven into lozenges quickly send down roots into the soil and become green after just a few weeks, delicately filtering the light. One need only look at the magnificent green architecture of the garden "Que vienne la pluie" (Let It Rain, 2016) to understand the aesthetic power of this use.

FACING PAGE Jean-Philippe Poirée-Ville, *Sylphes*, 2012.
PAGES 160–61 Rebecca Louise-Law, *Le Jardin préservé* (The Preserved Garden), 2017.

SPECTACULAR SCENARIOS AND STAGINGS

Each garden at Chaumont-sur-Loire invites visitors into a particular universe, framed by the form of the plots—a micro-landscape that is a concentrate of beauty and visual effectiveness, with the power to linger long in the memory. The constraints due to the small scale of the space force the designers to find unusual methods and original solutions that will surprise and win over the visitor by being immediately intelligible.

The surprise effect can develop into a powerful aesthetic emotion. This was the case with the glasshouse floating on water in the "Cheveux d'ange" (Angel Hair) garden (2010 festival), which made a real impact with its poetic winter garden filled with hanging tillandsia and its surreal white chairs sitting on the surface of the water, in a magical setting of aquatic plants.

Another scene that captured imaginations was "Les Belles aux eaux dormantes" (Sleeping/Floating Beauties; 2017 festival), where roses placed on the water dialogued with water lilies in the same pink color amid the highly graphic forms of rushes and horsetails. A metaphor for the impossibility of romantic relationships because of the separation of its elements, this garden, planted with roses chosen to ensure successive flowerings, charmed visitors throughout the duration of the festival, with the changing reflections of the sky and the clouds in the water adding to the magic of the scene.

The infinitely poetic "Réflexions" garden (2008 festival) presented the viewer with a pool of aquatic plants saturated with reflections brought about by a scintillating mesh made from a multitude of little, oscillating mirrors held above the water. A rusty-looking metal jetty had been built over the water, splitting in two this blank, dream-like scene and symbolizing the division of manmade landscapes.

"La Jetée" (The Jetty; 2013 festival) spectacularly evoked the multiplicity of prisms through which we perceive the real and the illusions caused by the excess of information in the digital age. Only the tip of the jetty allowed for serene contemplation, a reconciliation with the self, and an end to the dispersion of the senses.

"Voir les sons, entendre les couleurs" (2013 festival) lured visitors into an extraordinary cocoon, reached after moving through the heart of a space of sensory overload—a luxuriant setting planted with purple euphorbia and tree ferns and edged with mist.

"La Rivière des sens" (River of the Senses; 2013 festival) offered an initiatory journey along a river that was at once plant-based and architectural, where visitors lost all their bearings as the wooden frames that formed the arch around the path suddenly switched around, now being overgrown with foliage and strong perfumes. After a kind of heady dream, visitors emerged from this incredible sensory adventure with a feeling of peace.

"L'Envers du décor" (Behind the Scenes; 2011 festival) conjured up a surreal garden under a bubble, one that was rich with artificial flowers whose fascinating colors were an effective visual warning of the risk of losing plant species as a result of the overexploitation of nature and the globalization of taste.

The exotic garden of "Locus genii, le génie est partout" (Genius Loci, Genie Location; 2012 festival), punctuated with gardens and doors, inspired by the story of Aladdin, immersed visitors in an atmosphere straight out of the *Thousand and One Nights*, suggesting a place where the genie could rest, and that hid not just one, but dozens of magic lamps.

Surrounded by extraordinary mirrors, after visitors walked through an area that was exclusively green, "De l'autre côté du miroir" (Through the Looking Glass; 2017 festival) transported them into a fascinating universe, an infinite and vertiginous field of brightly colored flowers, multiplied ad infinitum, whatever the season.

FACING PAGE Rozenn Duley and Grégory Dubu,
"Pour l'amour de Tongariro" (For the Love of Tongariro), 2014.
PAGES 164–65 Christophe Marchalot, "Cheveux d'ange"
(Angel Hair), 2010.

Filled with haystacks with highly diverse forms, referencing all the European agricultural traditions, "Des meules impressionnantes" (2013 festival) carried visitors into the heart of a Renoir or Monet painting, set in an idealized and fragrant countryside.

Expressing both anger and jealousy, the "Pour l'amour de Tongariro" garden (For the Love of Tongariro; 2014 festival) evoked a Maori legend at the heart of an exotic landscape, featuring amorous volcanoes simply covered with stonecrops, slate, and mists, surrounded by abundant vegetation.

Joining art and flowers, the "Inspiration" garden (2017 festival), which suggested a painter's studio, offered the sight of various shifting landscapes seen through windows constructed by multiple wooden frames of varying dimensions.

Richly framed with gold, the pool in "Le Domaine de Narcisse" (The Domain of Narcissus; 2014 festival) held up a precious mirror to the luxuriant landscape around it.

"Fragment'ère" (Fragment'Era; 2008 festival) poetically related the way in which the fragmentation of the earth created biodiversity. Stone walls, green from the plants that had colonized them, plus an arrangement of volcanic stones ensured the transition from one level of evolution to another and symbolized the separation and drift of the continents.

The spectacular museum-garden "Réflexion d'un collectionneur" (Reflection of a Collector; 2015 festival) gave visitors the impression that they were entering a private enclosure displaying extraordinary paintings that were, in fact, the reflection of a hidden garden.

ABOVE Institut National d'Horticulture (Angers), "Fragment'ère" (Fragment'Era), 2008.
FACING PAGE Cathy Viviès and Vanessa Farbos, "L'envers du décor" (Behind the Scenes), 2011.

ABOVE Coline Giardi, Thomas Dalby,
Cléo Deschaintres, Ugo Elzière, Nicolas Suissa,
Léonard Cattoni, and Margot Chabert,
"La Rivière des sens" (River of the Senses), 2013.
RIGHT César Gourdon and Amélie Busin,
"La Jetée" (The Jetty), 2013.

THE ELEMENTS

Out of the four elements, we know, of course, that water has always played a major role in garden design. During the early years of the festival, this endlessly rich subject was the chosen theme on several occasions. Water is omnipresent in the gardens at Chaumont-sur-Loire, with pools and ponds reflecting the sky, waterfalls, various kinds of fountains, and aquatic effects of all kinds.

The form water has taken has been endlessly varied. For example, in 2017 there was the wonderful pool with graphic water effects on its surface by Alexis Tricoire, in "La Planète en ébullition" (The Planet in Turmoil) garden or the dreamlike pool with the floating glass-house in the "Cheveux d'ange" garden in 2017, or again the "devil's pond" in the "Pouvoir des sorcières" garden of the same year. And the "Vasques vives" (Living Urns; 2008 festival) showed that the perpendicular movement of the water increased its purification and its vivification. This dynamic cascade using waterfalls generated an incredibly clear wave.

"Le Jardin miroir" (The Mirror Garden; 2014 festival) in the Prés du Goualoup park reflected the sky and the giant leaves of the gunneras planted on the edge of the water, while the water in the "Jardin des nuées qui s'attardent" (Garden of Dallying Clouds; 2012 festival), by the great Chinese architect Wang Shu, reflected the clouds.

Cascades, canals, urns, basins, and even rice paddies with endlessly renewed or reinterpreted forms appeared in the plots, bestowing on the gardens the soothing or cathartic qualities of water.

Mist, too, has its part to play, and the designers readily make use of fogs and fumaroles, which bring a theatrical and dreamlike dimension to the gardens.

The designers embody the presence of air in numerous ways, with colored cloth fluttering in the wind, and various weathervanes and anemometers. They also use the suppleness of grasses that bend in the slightest breeze.

If fire exists only metaphorically, landscape artists are also skilled at playing on the multiple colors of the earth, whether dark or pale, ocher or red.

FACING PAGE Alexis Tricoire, "La Planète en ébullition" (The Planet in Turmoil), 2017.
PAGES 172–73 Anna Santacreu Felis, Armelle Renard, Dorothée Fischer, Louis Sicard, and Sergio Garcia Gasco Lominchar, "Le Jardin des couleurs captives" (The Garden of Captive Colors), 2009.

MATERIALS

At Chaumont-sur-Loire—a hive of unmatched inventiveness—the designers deploy all kinds of materials with incredible virtuosity in order to enrich their gardens. They merge and combine materials—wood, glass, stone, fabric, and metal.

At Chaumont, indeed, wood is used to edge the plots, to partition the kitchen gardens. Here designers sculpt with willow branches, build thickets with chestnut wood, create surprising chairs. They even make daring use of plastic so that its bold colors can triumph in the midst of the plants, asserting its yellows and oranges and the luminous transparency of this apparently incongruous material. Colored resins and polyesters also appear in the composition of these gardens.

And glass, as well, is used. Visitors will thus have seen magnificent balls of recycled glass in green or blue, or brilliant shards of shattered glass placed on the ground. But the transparency of glass can create superb and translucent walls whose reflections play with the daylight. Sometimes, transparent glass partitions are installed, and even low walls of recycled sunglasses and spectacles.

Also used are schist and slate, sand and terracotta, fragments of brick, old steel, and oxidized metal. Everything can be combined and mixed here. Earth, glass, wood, mirror glass, copper, and a thousand other materials have thus made their appearance in the gardens. Some designers have gone so far as to employ rubber tires, either whole or in scraps. The garden designers at Chaumont-sur-Loire are, of course, at the forefront of this inventive and challenging use of new materials.

Just think, for example, of the dazzling pinks stones of the "Éternelles Éphémères" (Eternally Ephemeral) garden (2017 festival), which contrasted magnificently with the surrounding plants. Or of the walls of volcanic stone in the "Fragment'ère" garden (2008 festival) and the accumulations of white rocks in the "Apis vertigo" garden (2017 festival). Or again the slate and schist floors of the "Jardin des émergences" (Garden of Emergencies; 2016 festival).

When it comes to glass, the fragments of crushed crystals concentrating rays of sun in the "La Halte des teinturiers" (The Dyers' Rest) garden (2009 festival); the balls of colored glass glowing at the feet of bamboos and shrubs; the translucent, finely worked partitions of the "Calligr-âme" garden (2010 festival), and the demijohns of the "Suspensions climatiques" (Climatic Suspension; 2015 festival) showed how useful glass can be to landscape designers. Indeed, they make frequent use of mirrors to enlarge their space and reflect the sky or flowers.

The playful plastic of the golden balls in the "Ma cassette" garden, the suspended glasses in the "Ultraviolet" garden (2014 festival), and the colored bubbles of the "Jardin Mange-tête" (2009 festival) provide other examples. The suspended plastic seeds of "Le Pollen exubérant" (Exuberant Pollen; 2011 festival) floated poetically, buoyed by the lightness of their synthetic material.

As for rusted metal, it can be made to provide walls and floors in the same colors as the earth that fit in magnificently with the green landscapes. In the "Gram(in)ophone" garden (2013 festival) there emerged from the ground a structure in oxidized metal whose vaulted top seemed to have been sculpted by the movements of the wind.

As for wood, not one year of the festival goes by without this timeless material being put to surprising uses.

ABOVE Jean-Pierre and Tangi Le Dantec, "Le Jardin de la terre gaste" (The Waste Land Garden), 2010.
RIGHT Charlotte Macé, Rémi Pernet-Mugnier, and Tanguy Sorre, "Le Voyage intérieur" (The Inner Journey), 2018.

ABOVE Swan Cazaux and Claire Dematos,
"Suspensions climatiques" (Climatic Suspensions), 2015.
FACING PAGE Noémie Chevereau, Frédérique Michel,
Dimitri Leduc, Frédéric Langel, Guillaume Felder,
Jean-François Clergeaud, and Luc Meinrad, "La Halte
des teinturiers" (The Dyers' Rest), 2009.

NEW TECHNIQUES, NEW CULTURES

Both contemporary techniques and the rehabilitation of ancient horticultural methods are sources of remarkable innovation in the work of the garden designers at Chaumont-sur-Loire. Chaumont is without doubt a place where ancestral techniques are revived—witness, for example, the use of raw earth as a building material, or that of *gabions*—metal crates filled with bricks or stones with which it is possible to build walls without the need for cement. Or again, one may see simple stake fences, which are a very useful way of surrounding gardens.

The "Jardin flottant du songe" by Jean-Philippe Poirée-Ville made use of original technical resources, such as a solar pump, which nourished this poetic, soilless garden created with hydroponic techniques. This involved a closed-circuit drip irrigation system and aeroponics, with the roots of the plants surrounded by water vapor.

Straw culture, which is very interesting in this respect, in that no earth is required for growing the plants, was used to create a kitchen garden in "Un paysage à goûter" (A Landscape for Tasting; 2013 festival). The landscape designers also developed original vertical designs with climbing plants such as hops supported by military mesh.

FACING PAGE Pascale Marq, Pierre-Marie Tricaud, Emmanuel Taillard, Laurence du Plessix, Baptiste Pierre, and Yann Le Yondre, "Un paysage à goûter" (A Landscape for Tasting), 2013.
PAGES 184–85 Joost Emmerik, "Le Jardin de la bière" (The Beer Garden), 2012.

RECYCLING
AND RECUPERATION

Chaumont-sur-Loire is a great center for the appropriation of everyday objects and transformation of used items, a place where they are given a new lease of life by garden designers, in ways that are sometimes surprising and always poetic. Among the materials converted in this way are industrial pallets, crates, and cases of all kinds, jute cloth, horticultural sheets, fishing nets, agricultural sheeting, bamboo tunnels, and umbrellas—to name but a few.

And if the year 2008 witnessed the realization of a famous "Jardin poubelle" (Trashcan Garden) by the landscape designers Christine and Michel Péna, made using all the remnants from the construction of the festival gardens, and coming across as a veritable manifesto in favor of recycling and respect for the environment, every year sees the Domain become the theater of some remarkable ideas. Take, for example, the astonishing wall of bottles, or wall of watering cans, that served as the shower room in "La Maison vivante" (The Living House; 2016 festival). We saw pallets standing like skyscrapers in the soilless urban garden called "Lucy in the Sky" (2011 festival). Trays became giant bulbs in "Les Bulbes fertiles" (Fertile Bulbs; 2011 festival), or accommodated a hen house in "Le Jardin des poules" (Hens' Garden; 2014 festival.) Accumulations of food cans were used as a new kind of container for plants in "Jardin mis en boîte" (Canned Garden; 2014 festival), and tires were assembled to create a new kind of soil in "Paradis inversé" (Reverse Paradise; 2014 festival).

ABOVE AND RIGHT Chilpéric de Boiscuillé, Raphaëlle Chéré, Pauline Szwed, and Benjamin Haupais, "Lucy in the Sky," 2011.

INNOVATIVE IDEAS

Think of the latest trends, all the current creations or inventions, and there is a fair chance they were seen first at Chaumont-sur-Loire, whose spirit of openness and readiness to experiment are well known to garden designers. For example, this was where "seed bombs" made their debut as part of "Explosive Nature" (2016 festival). An ancestral practice from Japanese agriculture, the role of the seed bomb is to help reinject nature into our environment and embellish our cities in a kind of horticultural guerrilla tactic. In the "Suspensions climatiques" garden, "terrariums," i.e., demijohns—green cabinets of curiosities and bubbles of greenery—displayed special compositions with maximum humidity levels, thereby reducing the need for watering.

Floating gardens, or kitchen gardens on the water, a reference to the crop cultures on Inle Lake in Burma, were a feature of the 2016 festival. In the "Que vienne la pluie" garden, they offered a solution both to rising water levels and to the loss of cultivable land. One year, a garden even used hundreds of little mirrors to capture the light and to illustrate metaphorically the over-information that afflicts contemporary societies.

FACING PAGE Loulou de la Falaise, "Le Jardin bijou" (The Jewel Garden), 2011.

ABOVE AND FACING PAGE Marguerite Ribstein
and Grégory Cazeaux, "Explosive Nature," 2016.

STRUCTURES OF ALL KINDS

As in all gardens, shelters, huts, climbing vines, bowers, pergolas, and crop shades flourish on the plots at Chaumont-sur-Loire, creating an endlessly varied interplay of shadow and light. You may see large numbers of huts, shelters, tables, mirrors, glasshouses, and verandas in all shapes, sizes, and materials. Their primary purpose, of course, is to protect the plants.

"À table" (Dinner's Served; 2015 festival), for example, featured a central glasshouse supporting a collection of extraordinary varieties of fruits and vegetables—black tomatoes, purple bell peppers, violet cauliflowers, white eggplants, fuchsia pink Swiss chard, climbing "spinach" etc., surrounded by flowers and grasses offering a gamut of textures and shapes, as surprising as they could be familiar.

"Suspensions climatiques" offered up a hanging garden, its levels overflowing with plants, and a labyrinthine structure filled by a jungle of plants that can survive without human intervention.

"Cabinets de curiosités végétales" (Cabinets of Plant Curiosities; 2015 festival) set out to create a museum-style setting for a collection of palm trees laid out in twelve alcoves.

"Le Collectionneur de l'ombre" (2015 festival) invited visitors to discover a collection of ferns on industrial-style shelving, adding up to a collection of materials with different natures and forms (stretched canvas, wooden decking, a metal grid, corrugated iron, trees with light foliage), bringing forth a great diversity of shadow and light effects.

"La Serre des victorias" (Victoria Amazonicas Glasshouse; 2016 festival) was created in order to present visitors with extraordinary aquatic plants such as the *Victoria amazonica*, whose big, tray-like leaves with raised sides need high temperatures.

As for the poetic hut of the floating garden "Que vienne la pluie," it invited visitors to rest awhile under its weave of living willow.

FACING PAGE Laure Le Gal, Pauline Goffin, and Olivia Frapolli, "Le Temple de nos pensées" (Temple of Our Thoughts), 2018.
RIGHT Youngjun Kim, "Le Filet de pensées" (The Netting of Thoughts), 2018.

ABOVE AND RIGHT The small glasshouse contains
a collection of tropical water lilies.
PAGES 198–99 Arthur Leveque de Vilmorin,
Romain Lacoste, and Paul Leurent, "Le Soulèvement
des graines" (Uprising of the Seeds), 2016.

EXTRAORDINARY FLOORS AND PATHS

In the limited gardening space offered by the festival, the ground tends to be intensively worked, with earth and sand in a huge array of colors, carpets of different materials, paving, gravel, sloping pebble surfaces, paths made of tree logs, wooden marquetry, or railway sleepers. Ground is also covered with more unusual materials, such as fragments of tiles and scraps of rubber or ground glass. Flooring contains inlays of naïve or highly worked mosaic, decorations in rocaille, and more.

All sorts of mulch, from the husks of cacao beans to flecks of linseed, beds of fern or ground pine, gravel ground-cover, or smashed tiles provide protection from evaporation and weeds.

The black and white gravel of the "Du noir de l'eau au blanc du ciel" garden (2009 festival) played a particular role in defining the meaning of the project. It made reference to the well-known Escher print depicting the gradual evolution from white to black.

The beige and black sands of the "Ocre Loire" (Loire Ocher) garden (2009 festival), in colors of slate and that recalled the riverbank, evoked the delicate Loire landscapes painted by Olivier Debré. As for the blue stones and gravel of the "La Biodiversité bleue" (Blue Biodiversity) garden (2011 festival), they resonated in a subtle dialogue with the blue-mauve of the plants.

At Chaumont-sur-Loire, visitors have sometimes found themselves walking on different types of bark or the brown shells of nuts or even peach stones. Often, the colors of the sawdust underfoot are chosen to echo the colors of the plants, as could be seen in the gardens "Les Belles aux eaux dormantes" (2017 festival) and "Voir rouge" (2009 festival).

But floors like the black tar of the "Résurrection, éloge de la défaillance" (Resurrection, in Praise of Failure) garden (2014 festival), happily overcome by plant life, or the sculpted cement of "Le Bouquet d'après" (The Bouquet Afterwards; 2017 festival) show that man-made materials also have their place in the festival gardens, if only to bring out the power of nature as it reasserts its rights.

LEFT AND FACING PAGE Ana Morales, "Résurrection, éloge de la défaillance" (Resurrection, in Praise of Failure), 2014.
PAGES 202-3 Sarah Chantrel, Valérian Goalec, Bruno Dubois, and Vincent Dupont-Rougier (École Régionale des Beaux-arts, Rennes), "Ocre Loire" (Loire Ocher), 2009.

DESIGN

Whether or not they are designers, those who conceive the gardens at Chaumont-sur-Loire work a great deal on inventing forms and coming up with new solutions, in terms both of furniture and of interior and exterior architecture. This exploration of possibilities and the invention of certain elements of furniture, which it might be possible to develop on a broader scale, is one of the characteristics of Chaumont-sur-Loire, where the inventiveness of the garden creators, who are often young and therefore, luckily, still "unformatted," is almost limitless.

In this way, original tables and chairs have seen the light of day, like the eccentric pieces of mirror-furniture of the "Vivre au jardin" (Living in the Garden) plot (2016 festival), which were almost invisible amid the vegetation that they nonetheless reflected in every direction. Or the huge white circular table that was set out in the "Bloom" garden (2014 festival), giving onto a magnificent and inaccessible garden, uniformly red in color. Also worthy of admiration were the unlikely, poetic white glasshouses of Russian dachas.

Every year, all kinds of seats are invented, whether simple lengths of wood, geometrically carved to make Patrick Jouin's benches, or artistically wrought wicker chairs ("Ma terre, mater;" 2010 festival).

FACING PAGE Camille Baudelaire and Élodie Dauguet,
"Vivre au jardin" (Living in the Garden), 2016.
ABOVE Collectif Moonwalklocal and Paysagistes sans
Frontières, "Le Livre de sable" (The Book of Sand), 2018.

ABOVE AND RIGHT Johan Laure, Hadrien Balalud de Saint Jean, and Guillaume Giraud, "Bloom," 2014.

BOTANY

The capacity for invention displayed by the different teams does not stop with the use of new materials. Plants are at the heart of the creative dynamics at Chaumont-sur-Loire.

In addition to the botanical experiments carried out by the Domaine when it creates and develops its numerous permanent gardens over the eighty acres of its site, the International Garden Festival brings to light plants that are no longer used or have been forgotten, or creates unprecedented combinations. This is all part of the special exercise that goes into creating a garden that—even if it lasts as long as six months—is ephemeral.

Some plants, like coral bells, which are interesting for their chromatic qualities—they go from purple to black, via brown and caramel—as well as for their hardiness, have made many appearances in the gardens in recent years. Ophiopogon, with their remarkable graphic qualities and extraordinary black color, also feature frequently in festival gardens. Ornamental grasses such as carex and miscanthus, among others, can be used to create scenes of remarkable fluidity by playing virtuoso games with the color, volume, and growth of these delicate and flexible plants. The accumulative effect of the use of tall grasses and the working up of the plant material give the gardens an incomparable lightness, delicacy, and suppleness, allowing the eye to feast on fascinating swathes of color that are vibrant with light. In recent years, too, there has become a fashion for new hydrangeas and stonecrops. What the festival gardens invite us to experience is thus an extraordinary universe devoted to the triumph of unexpected botanical combinations and color harmonies.

By way of an example, we may consider the plant combinations of the "Jardin des émergences" (2016 festival), where many spectacular Mediterranean plants, including yuccas, yarrows, coneflowers, cinquefoils, and santolinas, came together to sumptuous effect in a dry garden.

FACING PAGE La French Fine Fleur, "Jardin pluriel et singulier" (Plural and Singular Garden), 2017.

Other combinations included the Sarracenia in cages and the other flesh-eating plants of "Carnivore Parc" (2015 festival), which inspired visitors with the subtlety of their tawny browns and greens. The "Porte-bonheur" garden (2015 festival) presented a rich medley of clovers, with four-leafed species planted in soil and others in frames because of their alleged preciousness, and yet others, abundant but less well known, which are colored and go from brown to iridescent.

"Le Jardin de bougainvilliers" (The Garden of Bougainvilleas; 2015 festival) brought together an exceptional collection of purple, mauve, pink, red, and orange bougainvilleas, while the ferns of the "Le Collectionneur de l'ombre" garden (2015 festival) revealed just how multifarious the crenelated, smooth, and other forms of these plants can be. The specimens here came from specialist collections and nurseries little known to the public.

"L'Homme qui aimait les fleurs" (The Man Who Loved Flowers; 2017 festival) presented an extraordinary ensemble of blue flowers shown escaping from planters, with surprising blue passionflowers, sage, agapanthus, jasmines, speedwells, and stonecrops.

The "Jardin pluriel et singulier" (Plural and Singular Garden; 2017 festival), composed by a collective of nursery and horticulture specialists, showcased an anthology of acanthus, clematis, orchids, geraniums, lantana, phlox, and giant dahlias, while "Le Jardin des 101 pélargoniums" (The Garden of 101 Pelargoniums; 2015 festival) put forward a stunning collection of pelargoniums displaying an exceptionally diverse range of shapes, colors, and scents.

If "flower power" was the theme in 2017, flowers are naturally in power every year at Chaumont-sur-Loire, and their constantly renewed sublime, fragile, evanescent beauty is at the heart of the dream that is the International Garden Festival.

ABOVE Katarina Brandt, "Le Jardin des 101 pélargoniums" (The Garden of 101 Pelargoniums), 2015.
FACING PAGE Conservatory of Specialist Plant Collections, "Le Jardin des bougainvilliers" (The Garden of Bougainvilleas), 2015.
PAGES 212–13 Pierre Lavaud and David Simonson, "Jardin des émergences" (Garden of Emergences), 2016.

A MULTISENSORY EXPERIENCE

COLORFUL GARDENS

Gentle or dazzling, playing with light and its variations through the day, color is one of the keys to any garden. Not surprisingly, the designers of ephemeral gardens at Chaumont-sur-Loire are very much involved in considering the energy of color. Whether multicolored or monochrome, their creations make the most of every nuance of color.

In 2017, for example, visitors to the "Au pied du mur" (At the Foot of the Wall) garden were greeted by a polychrome space where hundreds of packets of seeds were displayed on the wall. The translucent jars of colors in "Jardin du teinturier" (The Dyer's Garden; 2015 festival) fascinated visitors with shimmering reflections, while the pastel linens of the "Lessive en fleurs" garden (2008 festival) are remembered by all who saw them.

Black, too, can be a color, as Chaumont has shown. In her extraordinary scheme, architect Odile Decq created a comprehensively dark floor out of mesmerizing black mirrors.

The "Résurrection, éloge de la défaillance" garden (2014 festival) exhibited an expanse of black concrete split open in the middle and gradually reclaimed by nature, while a floor in dark rubber and scraps from tires provided the setting for the "Paradis inversé" garden (2014 festival). If the color green is inevitably very prominent in Chaumont-sur-Loire, the thousand and one shades of green in the garden, where surreal suspended figures denoted blindness at the wrongs inflicted on nature by humankind, drew their power from the subtle pictorial work of the designers.

BELOW Agrocampus Ouest (Angers),
"La Biodiversité bleue" (Blue Biodiversity), 2011.
FACING PAGE Nicolas Stadler, Alice Stadler,
and Thierry Giraut, "De l'autre côté du miroir"
(Through the Looking Glass), 2017.

SOUND GARDENS

In addition to the birdsong, the croaking of frogs, and the murmur of cascading water, sound is never far from the gardens at Chaumont-sur-Loire. It could be found in the magnificent voice of Billie Holliday, emanating from a piano placed in a field of poppies, or in the original and powerful music that visitors could trigger in the extraordinary "Jardin à frôler" (2013 festival) simply by touching creepers fitted with ultra-sensitive sensors.

FACING PAGE Anna Zaragoza, Jasper Springeling,
Berno Strootman, and Matthijs Willemsen,
"Hommage à Lady Day," 2010.
RIGHT Alexandre Levy and Sophie Lecomte,
"Jardin à frôler" (Garden to Brush Against), 2013.
PAGES 222–23 Julie Aviron, Jérôme Levallard, Alice Gounet,
and Sarah Schrader, "Voir les sons, entendre
les couleurs" (See Sounds, Hear Colors), 2013.

PERFUMED GARDENS

In the "Apis vertigo" (2017 festival) garden the *Carlina acaulis* had visitors spellbound with its irresistible fragrance, while the heady perfume of the white jasmine along the pools in the "Levant" garden (2017 festival) transported them into a dream of the Orient.

Another year visitors could don *sniffettes* (2013 festival)—helmets that produced wild, disturbing, or sensual fragrances, which invited visitors to acquaint themselves with unusual perfumes. That same year visitors could also immerse themselves in the heady perfume of verbena in the "Ma terre, mater" garden, where they could sit in deep arm-chairs surrounded by thousands of little white flowers. Twice, famous perfumers have brightened the festival with their talent by creating gardens with heady perfumes: Jean-Claude Ellena with dizzying fragrances of lily-of-the-valley, iris, and heliotrope in his "Jardin du parfumeur" (Perfumer's Garden; 2016 festival), and Francis Kurkdjian, who perfumed the fountain in "Toi et moi, une rencontre" (You and Me, a Meeting; 2012 festival), a garden created by Nicolas Degennes.

FACING PAGE Nicolas Degennes, "Toi et moi, une rencontre" (You and Me, a Meeting), 2012.
ABOVE Jean-Claude Ellena, "Le Jardin du parfumeur" (Perfumer's Garden), 2016.

LIGHT AND THE GARDENS AT NIGHT

Nothing can beat light when it comes to magnifying the soul of a garden. When evening falls, everything becomes different: the perfumes, the colors, and the sounds all take on a new dimension. At Chaumont-sur-Loire, the gardens are lit up on summer nights.

In the silence of the evening, the breezes, the cries of the birds, and the croaking of the frogs give the garden a different feel. The perfumes, revived by the dusk, convey a singular feeling of calm to visitors, encouraging them to savor the present moment silently. And it is then that the magic of the luminous effects—with their richly colored lights—comes into play, transfiguring the gardens and giving them a mysterious beauty. Underlining the architecture of each garden, playing elegantly and poetically on the highly graphic structures and plants, the lighting installations create dream-like atmospheres of tremendous lyricism.

FACING PAGE Stefan Laport (Gartenlandschaft Berg & Co. GmbH), Joachim Würster, and H. Lorber (Baumschulerzeugnisse GmbH & Co. KG), "La Couleur des éléments" (The Color of the Elements), 2009.

ABOVE Erik Samakh, *Lucioles* (Fireflies), 2008.

HUMOR AND FANTASY

Humor, too, is part of the festival's DNA. One year, for example, visitors were greeted by a giant rabbit, and the festival has always liked to reach out with situations that are unusual, droll, and sometimes even absurd.

One way of doing this was by inviting visitors into the picturesque "Vilain Petit Jardin de Jean-Michel Vilain" (Jean-Michel Vilain's Villainous Little Garden; 2010 festival), a gentle caricature of the clutter and odds and ends found in most gardens, with sheds and shelters of all kinds and a host of amusing details.

"Le Trône de fleurs" (Throne of Flowers; 2017 festival) invited visitors to sit on a strange throne surrounded with pitchforks and pickaxes in a twist on the popular series *Game of Thrones*, offering a playful set-up in which everyone could be king or queen for a day.

One year, it was even possible to enter into the highly vegetal confessional of the "Jardin de pécheresses" (2014 festival) or contemplate the amusing accumulation of gold of Molière's miser Harpagon in the "Ma cassette" garden (2014 festival). In "Liberté, Égalité, Fraternité" (2012 festival), a British team also presented a wacky army of gnomes revolting against their gradual disappearance from gardens.

And it was, of course, entirely natural for visitors to Chaumont to see plants growing in shoes.

FACING PAGE Tony Balmé, Ingrid Saumur, Fabien David, Franck Boulanger, and Fabrice Ramalinghom, "Dix pieds sous terre" (Ten Feet Under), 2010.
ABOVE Jonathan Rouvillois, Julien Lamoureux, Louise Prulière, and Claire Tanguy, "Saute qui peut!" (Jump if You Can!) [detail], 2013.
PAGES 232–33 The Rabbit mascot of Chaumont-sur-Loire.

A FAIRYTALE WORLD

Since every garden at Chaumont-sur-Loire tells a story related to the annual theme, it is hardly surprising that their designers should often lead us into the world of fairytales, of the *Thousand and One Nights*, of Charles Perrault, of Hans Christian Andersen, and of other famous authors of fantasy stories.

The designers show unmatched inventiveness as they work with timeless settings, playing games with proportions or marvelous objects. There are many examples of these dreamlike scenarios, so loved by children and the young at heart, in the creations at Chaumont-sur-Loire.

Visitors have been able to enter the worlds of fairytale characters, such as that of the witches in the red and black garden "Le Pouvoir des sorcières" (2017 festival), which evokes the dwellings of these canny mediators between humankind and nature.

"Le Jardin de la Belle au bois dormant" (Sleeping Beauty's Garden; 2012 festival) attracted visitors into a sublime garden of thorny delights, where an unwise princess was plunged into a sleep of a thousand years.

The "À la recherche du lupin blanc" (In Search of the White Lupin) garden (2017 festival) was a nod to the world of Lewis Carroll and took visitors into an unexpected world, beyond everyday appearance, with surprise plant scenes. Like in *Alice in Wonderland*, a tunnel here made visitors seem to shrink to flower-height. Terraced seating gave them a chance to stop and contemplate a magnificent tableau of green and white. "Le Jardin bleu d'Absolem" (2012 festival) evoked another of Alice's adventures with a wonderful flight of blue butterflies. Meanwhile, the "Papillonnez" (Butterfly) garden (2017 festival) presented a three-dimensional staging of Hans Christian Andersen's tale *The Butterfly*, perfectly illustrating one of the aspects of "flower power": the ability that flowers have to charm both humans and butterflies with their beauty.

ABOVE Benjamin Henno, Karine Haudrechy, Johanès Montagne, Lucile Hamoignon, and Chen-Yu Zhou, "À la recherche du lupin blanc" (In Search of the White Lupin), 2017.
FACING PAGE Christian and Jérôme Houadec, "Le Jardin bleu d'Absolem" (Absolem's Blue Garden), 2012.

POETRY

Without a doubt, gardens are one of the most obvious places for the expression of poetry, that hidden soul of real life, which makes us come alive in the larger world. Their living beauty seems to bring back the freshness of our first emotions and remind us that the marvelous manifests itself to those with the eyes to see. Poetry is a way of living differently in time. So let us walk through the gardens of Chaumont-sur-Loire and share the inspired vision of Eric Sander.

PAGES 236–37 AND FACING PAGE Mist in the Prés du Goualoup park.
RIGHT From tulips to irises, the flowers at Chaumont-sur-Loire
have many different faces. Here, *Eremurus ruyter*
'Brutus' and *Camassia cusickii* grow in abundance.
PAGES 240–41 Solène Ortoli, Yoann Cardinaux, André Carsenat,
Gérald Havel, and Julie Rouxel, "Réflexion d'un collectionneur"
(Reflection of a Collector), 2015.

GREEN CARDS

"Green cards," given as invitations to those one might not always associate with the world of gardens, have been the starting point for some fascinating projects. Because, of course, you don't have to work full time in the world of plants to come up with original ideas and extraordinary gardens.

With this in mind, over the last ten years at Chaumont some admirable creations have been dreamed up by architects, designers, artists, and even a choreographer.

LANDSCAPE DESIGNERS
Michel Corajoud
Alexandre Chemetoff
Jacques Simon
Michel Racine
Florence Mercier
Michel Péna
Erik Borja
Leon Kluge
Yu Kongjian

BOTANISTS
Patrick Blanc
Alexis Tricoire

ARCHITECTS
Wang Shu
Odile Decq
Dominique Perrault

DESIGNERS
Patrick Jouin
Pablo Reinoso
Mathieu Lehanneur

ARTISTS
Anne and Patrick Poirier
Ernesto Neto
Christophe Cuzin

PERFUMERS
Jean-Claude Ellena
Francis Kurkdjian

CHOREOGRAPHER
Benjamin Millepied

CHEF
Alain Passard

FASHION/BEAUTY
Loulou de la Falaise
Christophe Robin
Nicolas Degennes

FACING PAGE Christophe Robin, "Beauty Garden," 2009.

A PROTEAN GARDEN

THE METAMORPHOSIS OF AN ESTATE

Since 2008 and the birth of the établissement public, an autonomous public body combining the château and the International Garden Festival, many new spaces and gardens have been created on the site.

The first thing that I felt needed to be added to the ensemble was a certain gentleness, a sensitive way of linking the farm and the château, previously separated by an ugly parking lot and flattened by the summer sun. The creation of the white spring gardens in 2009, with thousands of white bulbs (narcissi, tulips, etc.), and the summer gardens, in this historic park, whose lawns used to be seriously parched by the July and August sun, was the first stage. All development was now guided by the concern to smooth rough edges, to mask flaws, and to use plants as an ally to render everything pleasing to the eye. This enabled me to gradually transform the whole, giving the site a harmony which is very much part of the pleasure of visiting.

The reorganization of the farmyard, getting rid of the cars and planting *Magnolia grandiflora* to welcome visitors; the staggered rows of boxwood; the arrival of bamboo, of rhododendrons, of oleanders, and aucubas in pots helped soften the austerity of this thoroughfare. In 2010 the historic park was very subtly restored by Louis Benech, by replanting new trees and felling many old ones that were now dangerous, and creating both a pool, which extended the perspective along the Allée du Prince-Albert, and a terraced garden under the avenue of linden trees near the château. In 2010–11 the historic park was also abundantly planted with blue camas and narcissi by Louis Benech.

Given the strong polychromatic effect of the festival gardens, my approach was to fill the Domain with pastel-colored gardens. That is why the spring plantations are white, which brings a feeling of tranquility to the park, echoing as they do the light flowers of the chestnut trees. The white rose garden that I decided to have planted alongside certain buildings in the farmyard also now provides shade and airiness at the entrance to the Domain. The summer and autumn gardens, in contrast, are blue and mauve, made up mainly of sages, delphiniums, and simple fragrant surfinias. In September the dahlias, asters, and Indian lilacs take over from the summer flowers, seeing in the autumn with their marvelous pinks and mauves.

FACING PAGE Fumiaki Takano, "Le Jardin japonais" (The Japanese Garden), 2014.

ABOVE The children's garden, where visitors can relax.
FACING PAGE The experimental kitchen garden,
created in 2009, is a homage to biodiversity. Many
of the fruits and vegetables growing there had been
all but forgotten since the eighteenth century.

INTERSTITIAL GARDENS
AND NEW GARDENS

I took particular care over the metamorphosis and enrichment of the plants in what are known as the "interstitial" gardens between the festival plots. Their presence is vital when the gardens first open, for their bulbs, and particularly the hyacinths, tulips, and camas, offer a vigorous celebration of the transition from winter to spring. Carefully cultivated by the Domain's talented gardeners, they evolve with the seasons, adding their own delicate score to the elaborate symphony wrought by the imagination of the garden designers taking part in the festival.

The experimental kitchen garden was created in 2009 on the site of a garden based on the layout of the botanical garden in Padua. To me, it was important that this garden, cultivated in keeping with the general principles of organic agriculture, should display biodiversity within given species, presenting and stimulating a new interest in the vegetables of the late eighteenth century. A certain number of rigorous principles are applied here: the soil is not turned over, the fertilizers are also organic, and the earth is covered with mown grass to protect it from rain runoff and to reduce the frequency of weeding. The gardeners also encourage cooperation between herbs, flowers, and auxiliary pollinizing insects. The vegetables are cultivated using what is called the "lasagna" method or "sheet gardening" on this site, which also welcomes a wide variety of flowers and plants chosen for their culinary uses. Among the specimens found here are rocamboles (sand leeks), yacóns, yellow nutsedge, and other delicious but previously forgotten fruits and vegetables.

The children's garden, with its shelters, its green tunnels, and its learning areas wholly dedicated to children, was, it seemed to me, essential if we were to properly welcome our young visitors. A space for discovery and learning, it is also a haven of well-being and relaxation, heady with a wide variety of fragrances and atmospheres.

Created exclusively out of natural materials, this garden is all about discovery through the senses. Children enter via walkways covered with climbing plants, symbolizing the journey into another world. With planted areas in the shape of boats or leaves, the garden also evokes the journeys made by plants. The "nests," small cocoons woven from living willow, offer children places to rest, listen, or observe. The "big cabin," bristling with chestnut saplings, provides an area for reading and talking.

The very popular and recently restored Vallon des Brumes (Valley of Mists) is an extraordinary island of poetry in the middle of the Domain that transports visitors to far-away places. You could easily imagine yourself in Indonesia, such is the luxuriance of the vegetation and the sheer size of some of the leaves in this tropical atmosphere, which is heightened by the permanent mists and the waterfall, all creating an exotic and cool refuge during the summer heat. Tree ferns and plants from Southeast Asia, originally chosen by Patrick Blanc, enrich the promenade, down below the concrete staircase-tree built in the late nineteenth century.

Whatever the season, plants are at the heart of the Domain's concerns, not only in all the exterior gardens but also inside the château. I think it is important to create and develop this delicate green thread linking all the activities. That is why we have white orchids permanently adorning the private apartments of the château, and these are often complemented in spring and at Christmas by subtle creations made from leaves and flowers by talented floral stylists like Clarisse Béraud.

But the Domain also plays its role as a permanent inventor of vegetal forms, exemplified by the incredible plant chandeliers and extravagant gourds shown during the Splendeurs d'automne (Autumn Splendors) event.

PERMANENT GARDENS

In 2012, a new twenty-five-acre park, the Prés du Goualoup, was opened. This meadow was laid out by the landscape designer Louis Benech, who conceived a big circular promenade in the spirit of the paths traced out by Duchêne in the nineteenth century. He sculpted groves of trees, maintained a central meadow and, in keeping with the commission he had received, distinguished plots to house contemporary gardens related to the major garden traditions. Every year, the Domain invites different creators to landscape these. Since the inception of Goualoup, several gardens have been opened, offering contemporary takes on the Chinese, Japanese, Korean, and English gardening styles.

I felt it was important to offer, with these non-ephemeral gardens, a contemporary twist on the codes employed by the civilizations that raised the art of the garden to its zenith. That is why we have invited major Chinese landscape designers and architects such as Yu Kongjian and Wang Shu to work here. The latter was awarded the Pritzker Prize for architecture in 2012, the same year he conceived his "Jardin des nuées qui s'attardent" at Chaumont.

CHINESE GARDENS

When he created his garden in the Chinese spirit, "Hualu, Ermitage-sur-Loire," in 2012, the last thing Che Bing Chiu wanted—and it was the same for the people commissioning him—was to import a pale copy of a traditional garden or a soulless and impersonal recreation of a scholar's garden. He likes to quote Jing Hao, the great master of landscape painting in the era of the Five Dynasties (907–960), who wrote in his notes on the art of the brush: "If vital energy [qi] is passed only through external pattern and is dropped out of the image, then the image dies."

For him, the contemporary challenge for a Chinese garden was to get away from the constraints of tradition while drawing on the sources of classical culture and thus achieving a formal and spatial renewal of the architectonic vocabulary of landscaping. His garden, "Hualu, Ermitage sur Loire," revisits the spirit of the traditional garden with its pavilions made, not from stone, but using techniques and materials from the Loire Valley. Its central pool, rimmed with sculpted stones and reflecting the hill—a central feature in Chinese gardens—is edged by willows, black pines, wisteria, and sinensis roses, and transports visitors into the atmosphere of gardens in the Celestial Kingdom

In "Carré et Rond" (Square and Round; 2013 festival), the great landscaper Yu Kongjian revisited the fundamental concepts of the traditional Chinese garden, such as feng shui, in which he is an eminent specialist. An important architect as well as landscape designer, greatly concerned by the ecological problems that face his country, conscious of the loss of forests, of the exhaustion of phreatic groundwater, and of the destruction of agricultural land, his practice of landscaping seeks to combine great beauty with complete respect for the environment, offering a home on a human scale. This little garden, "Carré et Rond," signifying "Earth and Sky," is a contemporary reinterpretation of traditional Chinese gardens,

FACING PAGE Che Bing Chiu, "Hualu, Ermitage sur Loire," 2012.
PAGES 258–59 Yu Kongjian, "Carré et Rond" (Square and Round), 2013.

one which integrates the very contemporary question of the management of rainwater into the Chinese philosophical question of the garden. This extremely rich project is interested in man and nature, in the formal language of the curved line and square, in strategy taking on board the experience of the surrounding wall and the opening of the little within the big, and in a construction technique based on the use of excavated material and backfill.

The "Jardin des nuées qui s'attardent" was created in 2012 by Wang Shu. This structure, composed of crisscrossing pieces of wood, recalls the complex interweaving of birds' nests. As if somehow overturned, this fragile wooden structure has been gradually overgrown by the climbing plants that grow at its side, forming a kind of net to catch the clouds above.

Inside this garden, the surface of the water is like a mirror reflecting the poetic play of light and shadow, of static wood and leaves quivering in the wind. The clouds are reflected in this delicate pool and we like to imagine them being caught in the nest, which surrounds us and is also reflected.

This is a pause, a contemplative parenthesis that can be savored here in a mood of calm and serenity. We can let our imagination run free, enjoy thought and friendship, as we respond to the invitation extended to us in the garden's very name, *Tingyun ting* ("Garden of Dallying Clouds") which refers to a poem by Tao Yuanming, "Dallying Clouds," and which is a vibrant hymn to friendship.

Time is a major element in gardens as it is in our lives, whatever our culture. The garden created by the Museum of Chinese Gardens in Beijing is a reflection on eternity. It recalls the Möbius strip, a Western symbol of infinity, a band whose compact surface has an edge that is homeomorphic to a circle, which means that it has only one side, unlike a standard band, which has two.

It also refers to yin and yang. In Chinese philosophy yin and yang (*tàijí tú*) are two complementary categories that are also linked to infinity. The yin corresponds, among other things, to the female principle, to the moon, to darkness, to freshness, to receptiveness. As for the yang, it represents essentially the masculine principle: the sun, luminosity, warmth, élan. This duality can also be associated with many other complementary oppositions: suffering and pleasure, aversion and desire, agitation and calm.

KOREAN GARDEN

A meditation on the fundamental elements of the Korean garden, this garden draws visitors into a poetic reverie.

From the fourteenth century, during the Choson era, the Korean art of the garden developed differently from that of other Asian gardens. This is because Korean gardens have singular structures that can be classified in three categories: tiered terraces, pools, and geometrically shaped islands—two-part compositions forming, respectively, an interior garden and an exterior garden.

These structures reflect a concept that is specific to Korean culture, in which the garden is a mythic place and a great receptacle of the void.

With its central pool, planted with lotus flowers, with its terraced gardens planted with pink azaleas, its mauve hibiscuses and its collection of traditional pottery, the Korean garden at Chaumont-sur-Loire subtly transports visitors into the Land of the Morning Calm.

JAPANESE GARDENS

This ensemble of Japanese gardens developed around the garden by Shodo Suzuki, "The Archipelago," which is the only work this great landscape designer created outside his native Japan. Representing the Japanese archipelago with these black stones placed—with Suzuki's agreement—on the water (in 1994 they were placed on sand), this garden envelops us in a poetic meditation on landscape. The landscape designer Fumiaki Takano later invented, in liaison with the great Japanese master, a very fine circular project, enclosing the work by Shodo Suzuki and tripling the area of the water mirrors reflecting the clouds.

ENGLISH GARDEN

If there is a country where the art of the garden plays an essential role, it has to be England. In the eighteenth century, it was the English garden that challenged the symmetry of classical parks with their trees pruned into cones, balls, and pyramids.

English landscape gardeners got rid of walls, hedges, and other forms of enclosure and opened gardens wide onto the surrounding landscape, onto the horizon, thereby transforming the whole of nature itself into a garden.

Vegetation that seems not to be controlled spreads in harmony with the scene, changing with the seasons and times of day. Unlike the French garden, the English garden sets out to imitate nature; rather than dominate it, it likes to give an impression of disorder, letting the imagination run wild. What is sought is the equilibrium of volumes, the harmony of colors, and the diversity of plant textures.

The English garden at the Prés du Goualoup, which we created in 2016, comprises, in the same spirit, mixed borders, alleys of roses and clematises on hoops bending under their load of fragrant flowers, curved paths, and luxuriant blue and pink beds, all immersing visitors in a poetic contemporary reinterpretation of the constants in the English garden.

FACING PAGE The Korean garden made by the Domain's gardeners in 2015.
PAGES 264–65 Shodo Suzuki, "The Archipelago," 2013.

BELOW A contemporary take on the English garden by the Domain's gardeners.

CONTEMPORARY ART IN ARCHITECTURE AND LANDSCAPE

INTRODUCTION

Everything about Chaumont-sur-Loire points to the connections between heritage, gardens, and artworks. These are force fields that visitors, even uninformed ones, can somehow sense. If, since 1992, the Domain of Chaumont-sur-Loire has been a prized site in the world of gardens, since 2008 the determination of the Région Centre-Val-de-Loire has also made it an art center where, every year, visitors discover new works, new installations, and new exhibitions. This openness to the visual arts and photography constitutes an important new period in the history of the Domain.

Chaumont-sur-Loire is a center for art and nature. All the works shown or created here have a connection with nature, in that they play with the landscape or make use of its elements and materials.

Artists invited to intervene in the château, in its outbuildings, or in its grounds, can sense the vibrations of the place and subtly bring out its memories and beauty. Everything unfolds in an ingenious harmony between styles and periods, between the memory of humans and that of the walls, between the radically contemporary interventions of certain artists and history, in a delicate dialogue with the architecture, settings, and trees from times past.

Visitors will respond, consciously or unconsciously, to the refinement of the chromatic, aesthetic, and historical connections, to the subtle affinities between the arts, between different ages, which bestow on the ensemble a secret graciousness, an absolute harmony that words cannot always explain. The visit is, above all, a sensorial experience.

Art and artworks reflect back the imaginary worlds, reveal the deep soul of the Domain, with an incredible poetic intensity, and artists give these timeless spaces the feel of a paradise restored. A place for sharing art, the Domain of Chaumont-sur-Loire, with its château, its grounds, and its gardens, is an unusual site, in terms both of its spaces and its program, which manages to touch members of the public from very different backgrounds and cultures, from the well informed to the complete newcomer.

Artists occupy spaces in the estate's outbuildings, as if these were pavilions that had been added on over the years (stables, farm, barns, the Fenil gallery, gallery of the gardeners' courtyard, the donkey stables, and unexpected parts of the château such as the kitchens, and the servants' and guests' rooms, previously hidden from the sight), but also the big parks, where they create contemporary constructions or follies that create a dialogue with the landscape.

What is important here is respect for the spirit of place; what counts, is the fact that each artist relates to the architecture and the natural setting—and that, every time, a new artistic adventure gives poetry precedence.

SPECIAL COMMISSIONS FOR CHAUMONT-SUR-LOIRE
These works are conceived for the Domain of Chaumont-sur-Loire and echo the grounds, the river, the landscape, the outbuildings, and the apartments in the château. The relationship established by the artists with the place stems from an understanding that is at once intuitive and profound, as if they immediately grasped all its mysteries and vibrations.

PAGES 268–69 Nils-Udo, *Volcan* (Volcano), 2018.
FACING PAGE *Idee di pietra – 1303 Kg di luce* (Ideas of Stone—1303 kg of Light) by Giuseppe Penone (2012).
PAGES 272–73 Sara Favriau, *J'ai remonté le temps y avait rien à faire. Les mêmes carrosses en bois à toute allure* (I went back in time, there was nothing to do. The same high-speed wooden carriages), 2017.

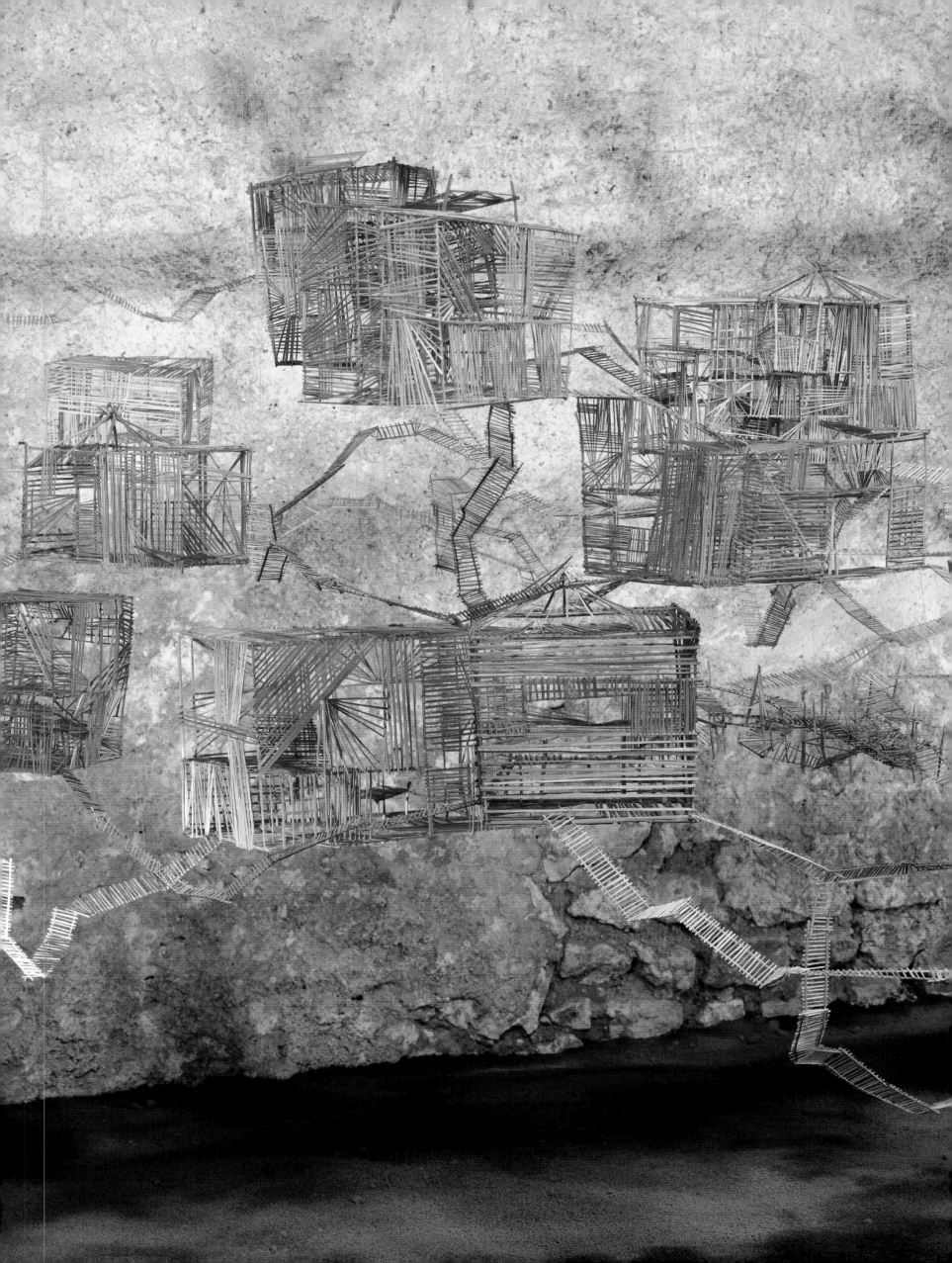

A UNIQUE EXPERIENCE
OF ART AND NATURE

The positioning of the artworks on show at Chaumont-sur-Loire is never by chance. Each work must be exactly where it stands, whether inside or outside, and could be nowhere else. The siting of the work is decided following intense conversations with the artist and is an essential part of the echo that it will set up with its surroundings. All the works—-and this is a fascinating task for me as a curator—are carefully presented, so as not to impair the magic of the site. A secret link is woven—has been woven—between each artist and each place, giving the impression that the installations have been present for much longer. The interdependence between the work and the site effectively plays an important role in the perception and resonance of the works created on-site.

In the same way, what is specific to the visitor's experience at Chaumont is the time-less, unchanging relation to the landscape. When walking round, visitors have the chance to experience the works corporeally, and this "incorporation" allows for a better ingestion, a better absorption of art by the soul, whatever the viewer's level of culture and knowledge of art.

Art, architecture, and nature thus transform the body and mind through an ineffable and secret alchemy. The visitor's progression is as much spiritual as it is visual.

Vincent Barré, *Chaos*, 2014.

A POETIC UTOPIA

Chaumont-sur-Loire is not a tourist site—it is a place of culture, in the deep sense of the word, in that it liberates and broadens the viewer's horizons, through the relation that it creates both with landscape and with an invisible world that lies beyond the artworks.

Chaumont-sur-Loire is a utopian place. It is, in a sense, a place of resistance to materialism, to the excesses and violences of contemporary society.

The site grows out of the idea that one can combine landscape, art, and history and offer the visitor a pause outside of time, an interlude of art, knowledge, and harmony. In such a place visitors can find beneficial reinvigoration and the possibility of replenishing their store of energy and poetry.

Poetry is master at Chaumont-sur-Loire and constitutes the common denominator of the artworks presented here. This is evident in the *Tremblements de ciels* (Trembling of Skies) devised by Marc Couturier; the incredible *Envoûtements* (Bewitchings) conceived by Sheila Hicks, under the château vaults; or the *Fleurs fantômes* (Phantom Flowers) revealed by Gabriel Orozco. We admire ponds of dandelions from the imagination of Duy Anh Nhan Duc in *Champ céleste* (Heavenly Field), and the *Herbiers d'or* (Golden Herbariums) concocted by Marie Denis and the hanging gardens created by Rebecca Louise Law. We contemplate a *Recinto sacro* (Holy Enclosure) in glass and crystal by Andrea Branzi, a *Nid des murmures* (Nest of Murmurs) by Stéphane Guiran, and a mysterious *Volcan* (Volcano) by Nils-Udo, hiding eggs in white marble. We discover a *Granges aux abeilles* (Bee Barns) and an *Arbre aux échelles* (Ladder Tree) by François Méchain; doorways to the unknown, such as *Le Passage* by Cornelia Konrads; a chapel enchanted by the work of Gerda Steiner and Jörg Lenzlinger; *Petite Loire* (Little Loire) in marble by Mathieu Lehanneur; a golden ball *En plein midi* (In the Heart of the South) by Klaus Pinter; and more.

All these works, these images, and these words resonate in the imaginary and leave a deep trace. They touch people's souls and offer them the "elsewhere" that they crave, if only for a few hours.

FACING PAGE Stéphane Guiran, *Le Nid des murmures* (Nest of Murmurs), 2017.

ABOVE AND FACING PAGE Duy Anh Nhan Duc,
Champ céleste (Heavenly Field), 2018.
PAGES 286–87 Fujiko Nakaya, *Standing Cloud*,
Cloud Installation #07240, 2013.

NATURAL MATERIALS

The Centre d'Arts et de Nature in Chaumont-sur-Loire is a place for the celebration of nature and its materials.

But if all the materials used by artists at Chaumont-sur-Loire come from natural elements, they are also highly diverse.

We see the wood in the works of Armin Schubert and Ursula von Rydingsvard, branches and twigs used by Cornelia Konrads and Bob Verschueren, woven arches of willow by Patrick Dougherty, *Les Racines de la Loire* (The Roots of the Loire) by Nicolay Polissky, made from vine stocks, but also the oak giants by Christian Lapie, and the pine cabins, walks, and promontories by Tadashi Kawamata.

But metal is not absent either, providing that it evokes the symbols and mysteries of nature. It appears in works created on-site here, like those of Abderrahim Yamou, and the various iterations of *Banc délirant* (Wild Bench) by Pablo Reinoso.

Also to be found are the wool, fibers, and fabrics of Sheila Hicks, and the immaculate cotton of Simone Pheulpin.

One of the poorest of poor materials, cardboard is valued material for artists, whether in the spectacular forests created by Éva Jospin, or in the fascinating waves representing different sounds by Andrea Wolfensberger.

Stone, slate, and marble are also present, notably in the historic park, with the phantasmagorical *Folie* (Folly) created by Éva Jospin, the powerful *Cairn* by Andy Goldsworthy, and the *Œil de la mémoire* (Eye of Memory), *Capella dans la clairière* (Chapel in the Clearing), and the *Fauteuil* (Armchair), in black or pale marble, by Anne and Patrick Poirier. The wonderful *Petite Loire* in green marble by Mathieu Lehanneur even flows in the stable courtyard.

Others prefer the floral, vegetal material of gardens. Herman de Vries has created a fabulous lavender carpet, a work as olfactory as it is visual, placed in the manège, while Gerda Steiner and Jörg Lenzlinger have conceived a fantastical garden in the chapel of the château: *Les Pierres et le Printemps* (Stones and Springtime). But Rebecca Louise Law, with her work comprising seventy-five thousand flowers hanging under an awning in the stables, and the fascinating *Champ céleste* by Dhuy Anh Nhan Duc, comprising thousands of graceful dandelions, also play with the infinitely delicate and fragile elements that are flowers and their corollas.

Some play with air and breath, as does Klaus Pinter with his fine, translucent, and gilded floating sculptures; others use water, like Erik Samakh, who conceived an extraordinary water mirror in the manège. As for Fujiko Nakaya, she summoned mist to create a constantly changing artwork that sculpts and enchants the landscape with a cloud that, whatever the time of day, remains constant.

PAGES 292–93 Christian Lapie, *La Constellation du fleuve* (The Constellation of the River), 2015.
RIGHT Pablo Reinoso, *Banc délirant* (Wild Bench), 2012.
PAGES 296–97 Tadashi Kawamata, *Cabane dans les arbres* (Tree House), 2011.

LEFT Nikolay Polissky, *Les Racines de la Loire* (The Roots of the Loire), 2014.
PAGES 300–01 Patrick Dougherty, *Untitled*, 2012.

ABOVE AND RIGHT Yamou, *Lien infini* (Infinite Link), 2016.

CIRCLES AND SPHERES

Echoing the shape of the château's towers, many of the works shown at Chaumont-sur-Loire put the emphasis on circular or spherical form in a kind of sacred geometry, each with its own vibrant power. That is the case with *Recinto sacro*, in glass and crystal, by Andrea Branzi, and with *Carbon Pool*, Chris Drury's incredible whirlwind of poplar trees burned at the center. It was the case with the interior and exterior installations in sequoia by David Nash, which refer to his famous *Ash Dome* in Wales, a circle of the eponymous trees that echoes the secret and fascinating form of the vortex. Then there is the figure of the lemon-squeezer, *Presse-citron*, a contemporary form by Betty Buy, or the germinations of *Sub-ex-terre* by Armin Schubert. There is the form of the golden ball by Klaus Pinter in the manège. The circle is the form of the earth, and that of stars and flowers. It is also a symbol of the infinity and circularity of the seasons and of life. It symbolizes time and eternity. The sky, the sun, and divine breath are represented by a circle, infinitely replayed by artists, through the ages, and notably by all those who are close to nature.

FACING PAGE A musician in front of a work by Klaus Pinter,
En plein midi (In the Heart of the South), 2018.

LEFT Armin Schubert, *Objets sphériques*
(Spherical Objects), 2013.
BELOW Chris Drury, *Carbon Pool*, 2014.

THE TRIUMPH OF COLOR

Over the years, certain colors have come to dominate the artworks amidst the symphony in green major played by the actual grounds at Chaumont-sur-Loire. Note, of course, the importance and omnipresence of the color of wood and earth: brown. But white, red, and gold also have their place in this dialogue with the surroundings and amongst themselves: they discreetly echo one another from one space and year to another.

ABOVE Sheila Hicks, *Glossolalia*, 2017.
FACING PAGE Sheila Hicks, *Sens dessus dessous* (Topsy Turvy), 2018.

ON ECOLOGY

Many of the works created at Chaumont-sur-Loire have an ecological resonance or meaning, for the artists invited to create them—often more than others—deeply feel the need to celebrate the earth and its marvels, which are so brutally threatened, or even destroyed nowadays by the uncontrollably fast evolution of modern societies.

This particular relation with art and landscape acts on the visitor's perception, through all the senses, of the site and the works, and spreads through their minds an awareness of the fragility of beings and things.

El Anatsui—a Ghanaian artist based in Nigeria and honored by the international art world's most prestigious prizes—created a fascinating gold and silver tapestry, *XiXe*, which is installed in the Fenil gallery, and made with reclaimed materials found in African waste dumps. Even if it is not at the heart of the artist's message, it is clear that the transmutation of materials at the heart of the work challenges us to think about the constant waste and uglification of our planet.

In the same way, *Ugwu*, a hill created in the historic park by the same artist, poetically reuses waste and wooden logs, usually discarded as trash.

While the Finnish artist Antti Laitinen came up with a suit of armor for a tree needing to defend itself against attacks by men, François Méchain expressed the suffering of forests with a spectacular work titled *L'Arbre aux couteaux* (The Tree of Knives) placed on the red sand of the manège, just as the Japanese artist Shigeko Hirakawa denounced acid rain and the massive bleaching of leaves. More than a theoretical discourse, the subtlety of a poetic work of art has a surer chance of touching minds and hearts, by helping to celebrate the beauty of the world as well as its extreme fragility.

FACING PAGE Shigeko Hirakawa, *L'Arbre aux fruits célestes* (The Tree with Heavenly Fruit), 2012.
PAGES 314–15 Antti Laitinen, *L'Arbre-chevalier* (The Knight Tree), 2015.

INDEX OF NAMES, ARTWORKS, AND GARDENS

Page numbers in italic correspond to captions.

A

"À la recherche du lupin blanc" (2017) 234, *234*
"À table" (2015) 195
Agrocampus Ouest Angers, school *128, 133, 218*
Ahmad Shah Qajar 64
Ailleurs, ici (2011) 10
Alfonso XIII, King of Spain 64
Allain, Mathieu *127*
Amboise, Charles I d' 22, 52
Amboise, Charles II d' *20,* 22, *22,* 52, *54*
Amboise, Georges d' *20,* 22, *22,* 52, *54*
Amboise, Pierre I d' *19,* 22
Anastazia (2017) *318*
Anatsui, El *309,* 312
Andersen, Hans Christian 234
"Apis vertigo" (2017) *133, 174,* 225
Aramon, Count d' *9, 19, 95*
"Arbre aux fruits célestes, L'" (2012) *312*
"Arbre-chevalier, L'" (2015) *312*
"Arche de Linné, L'" (2015) *127, 128*
Arthur, Jules *108*
"Au pied du mur" (2017) 215
Austria, Maria-Theresa d' *71*
Auvergne, Anne d' *26*
Aviron, Julie *221*

B

Balalud de Saint Jean, Hadrien *206*
Balayn, Carine *116*
Balmé, Tony *231*
Banc délirant (2012) *289, 294*
Bardin, Romain *113*
Bardon, Gaël *118*
Bardon, Georges 50, 76
Barré, Vincent *280*
Bartolazzi, Lorenza *215*
Baudelaire, Camille *205*
Baudelaire, Charles *141*
Beaubreuil, Laurent *128*
"Beauty Garden" (2009) *242*
Beccari, Eugenio *215*
"Belles aux eaux dormantes, Les" (2017) *163,* 200
Benech, Louis *92, 103,* 108, *249,* 256
Béraud, Clarisse 256
Bernhardt, Sarah 64
Berthier, Stéphane *107*
Bertin, Pauline *144*
"Biodiversité bleue, La" (2011) *200, 218*
Blanc, Patrick *81, 158, 242, 255*
Blancpain, Timothée *108*

"Bloom" (2014) 205, *206*
Bodin, Oriane *128*
Boille, Marcel *19*
Boiscuillé, Chilpéric de *188*
"Bon thé bon genre" (2010) *108,* 154
Bonnard, David *215*
Bonnaud, Xavier *107*
Bonneval, Karine *41*
Borja, Erik *242*
Boucher, Clément *107*
Boulanger, Franck *231*
Boutot, Emma *141*
Brandt, Katarina *150, 210*
Branzi, Andrea *282,* 304
Brittany, Anne of *67*
Broglie, Jacques de *26*
Broglie, Prince Henri Amédée de *10, 19, 32, 37, 43, 50, 52, 61, 76,* 64, *64, 67, 81, 95, 101*
Broglie, Princess de (see also Say, Marie-Charlotte-Constance) *10, 19, 32, 37, 50, 52, 61, 64, 67, 81, 101*
"Bulbes fertiles, Les" (2011) *107, 187*
Busin, Amélie *168*
Buy, Betty 304

C

Cabane dans les arbres (2011) *294*
"Cabinets de curiosités végétales" (2015) 195
Caillaud, Philippe *108*
Cairn (2016) *277,* 289
"Calligr-âme" (2010) *174, 174*
Campos, Ricardo Walker *136*
Carbon Pool (2014) 304, *307*
Cardinaux, Yoann *239*
Carlantonio, Barbara di *215*
"Carnivore Parc" (2015) *127, 127,* 210
Carolus I, King of Romania 64
Carolus-Duran 64
"Carré et Rond" (2013) 256, *256*
Carrol, Lewis *144,* 234
Carsenat, André *239*
Catherine the Great, Empress of Russia *71*
Cattoni, Léonard *168*
Cau, Niccolò *136*
Cazaux, Swan *180*
Cazeaux, Grégory *192*
Chabert, Margot *168*
Chamisso, Adelbert von *57*
Champ céleste (2018) *282, 284,* 289
Changeux, Jean-Pierre *108*
Chantrel, Sarah *200*

Chaos (2014) *280*
Charles I, King of Portugal 64
Charles IX *26, 29*
Chemetoff, Alexandre 242
Chéré, Raphaëlle *188*
Chevalier, Manon *113*
Chevereau, Noémie *180*
"Cheveux d'ange" (2010) *163, 163, 171*
Chikuunsai IV, Tanabe *277*
Chiu, Che Bing 92, 256, *256*
Christie, William *108*
Clement VII, Pope *26*
Clergeaud, Jean-François *180*
Cloud Installation #07240 «Standing Cloud» (2013) *284*
Coineau, Mathilde *144*
"Collectionneur de l'ombre, Le" (2015) *127, 195,* 210
Collective of nursery and horticulture specialists 210
Connexion/La source (2018) *277*
Constant, Benjamin *57*
Constellation du fleuve, La (2015) *294*
Corajoud, Michel *242*
Costanzo, Cristiana *215*
"Couleur des éléments, La" (2009) *149, 226*
"Coulisse d'un festin" (2012) *144, 144*
Couturier, Marc *282*
"Cuisine africaine" (2015) *113*
Currey, Ruth *174*
Cuzin, Christophe 242

D

Dalby, Thomas *168*
Dalcant, Thierry *144*
Dauguet, Élodie *205*
David, Christelle *128*
David, Fabien *231*
"De l'autre côté du miroir" (2017) *166, 218*
Debré, Olivier 200
Decq, Odile *215,* 242
Degennes, Nicolas *225, 225,* 242
Delage, Marion *144*
Dematos, Claire *180*
Demoisy, Lélia *120*
Denis, Marie *61, 282*
"Des meules impressionnantes" (2013) *141, 141, 166*
Deschaintres, Cléo *168*
Deval, Marguerite 64
Dias, Francesco Jacques *136*
Dietschy, Dorian *116*
"Dix pieds sous terre" (2010) *231*
"Domaine de Narcisse, Le" (2014) *136, 136, 166*
Dougherty, Patrick *289, 299*

Drury, Chris 304, *307*
"Du noir de l'eau au blanc du ciel" (2009) *149, 150,* 200
Dubois, Bruno 200
Dubu, Grégory *163*
Duchêne, Henri *9, 16,* 64, *92, 95, 95, 97, 103,* 256
Dugard, Claire *128*
Duley, Rozenn *163*
Dupont-Rougier, Vincent 200
Duraysseix, Olivier *107*
Duy Anh Nhan Duc *282, 284,* 289

E

Echenoz, Jean *108*
Edward VII, King of England 64
Ehrler, Joachim *81*
Elizabeth, Queen of Spain *26*
Ellena, Jean-Claude *225, 242*
Elziere, Ugo *168*
Emmerik, Joost *183*
En plein midi (2018) *81, 282, 304*
"En vert" (2012) *144, 144*
"Envers du décor, L'" (2011) *163, 166*
Escher *149,* 200
Eudes I, Count of Blois *19*
"Explosive nature" (2016) *190, 192*

F

Falaise, Loulou de la *190,* 242
Farbos, Vanessa *166*
Favriau, Sara *270*
Felder, Guillaume *180*
"Filet de pensées, Le" (2018) 195
Fischer, Dorothée *171*
"Fleur du mal" (2017) *133*
Fireflies (2008) *228*
Folie (2018) *289, 289*
"Forêt alimentaire" (2016) *122*
Forêt, Marie *154*
"Fragment'ère" (2008) *166, 166, 174*
François II, King of France *29, 46*
François III, Duke of Brittany *26*
Franklin, Benjamin *19, 71, 71*
Frapolli, Olivia 195
French Fine Fleur, La *209,* 210

G

Gantoin, Fabien *107*
Garcia Gasco Lominchar, Sergio *171*
Gaulejac, Byung-Eun Min de *133*
Gauric, Luc *26*
Gayou, Aline *144*
Giardi, Coline *168*

Giraud, Guillaume *206*
Giraut, Thierry *218*
Glossolalia (2017) *310*
Goalec, Valérian 200
Gobert, Patrice *144, 150*
Godde, Robin *141*
Godefroy, Marie-Éléonore *57*
Goffin, Pauline 195
Gold and Empire Herbarium (2017) *61*
Goldsworthy, Andy *277,* 289
Gounet, Alice *221*
Gourdon, César *168*
"Gourmanderie" (2014) *136*
"Gram(in)ophone" (2013) *174*
Guanaschelli, Francesca Romana *136*
Guéret, Delphine *128*
Guiran, Stéphane *282, 282*

H

"Halte des teinturiers, La" (2009) *174, 180*
Hamoignon, Lucile *234*
Hannibal *44,* 62, *62*
Hao, Jing 256
Haudrechy, Karine *234*
Haupais, Benjamin *188*
Haute culture (2014) *136*
Havel, Gérald *239*
Heckmann, Ulli *91*
Henno, Benjamin *234*
Henry II, King of France *19, 26, 46*
Henry III, King of France *26, 29*
Henry IV, King of France *26*
Héricault, Charles d' *57*
Hicks, Sheila *282,* 289, *310*
Hirakawa, Shigeko 312, *312*
Holiday, Billie *154,* 221
"Hommage à Lady Day" (2010) *154, 221*
"Homme qui aimait les fleurs, L'" (2017) *133, 133,* 210
Hopquin, Adèle *120*
Hostiou, Olivier *154*
Houadec, Christian *234*
Houadec, Jérome *234*
Hualu, Ermitage sur Loire (2012) *92,* 256, *256*
Hugonnier, Violaine *215*

I

Iannace, Eufemia *215*
Idee di pietra - 1303 kg di luce (2012) *270*
"Igloolik ultima" (2010) 154
"Inspiration" (2017) *166*
Institut national d'horticulture *166*
Isabella II, Queen of Spain 64
Istoc, Cristina *215*

J

J'ai remonté le temps y avait rien à faire. Les mêmes carrosses en bois à toute allure (2017) *270*
"Jardin à frôler, Le" *141, 221, 221*
"Jardin bijou, Le" (2011) *190*
"Jardin bleu d'Absolem, Le" (2012) *144, 234, 234*
"Jardin d'amour, Le" (2013) *141*
"Jardin de la Belle au bois dormant, Le" (2012) 234
"Jardin de la bière, Le" (2013) *183*
"Jardin de la terre gaste, Le" (2010) *178*
"Jardin déchêné, Le" (2014) *113*
"Jardin des 101 pélargoniums, Le" (2015) 210, *210*
"Jardin des bougainvilliers, Le" (2015) 210, *210*
"Jardin des couleurs captives, Le" (2009) *171*
"Jardin des émergences, Le" (2016) *122, 174,* 209, *210*
"Jardin des graines, Le" (2015) 127
"Jardin des nuées qui s'attardent, Le" (2012) *171,* 256, 261, *261*
"Jardin des pécheresses, Le" (2014) *136,* 231
"Jardin des poules, Le" (2014) 187
"Jardin des voyelles, Le" (2018) *244*
"Jardin du parfumeur, Le" (2016) *225, 225*
"Jardin du teinturier, Le" (2015) *116,* 215
"Jardin flottant du songe, Le" (2016) *122, 122,* 158, 183
"Jardin mange-tête, Le" (2009) *149, 174*
"Jardin miroir, Le" (2014) *103, 171*
"Jardin mis en boite, Le" (2014) 187, *187*
"Jardin pluriel et singulier" (2017) *209,* 210
"Jardin poubelle" (2008) 187
"Jardin préservé, Le" (2017) *158*
"Jardin qui se savoure, Le" (2016) *122*
Je reste (2016) *120,* 122
Jetée, La (2013) *163, 168*
Jospin, Éva *289, 289*
Jouin, Patrick 205, 242
Julhiet-Détroyat, Corinne *122*

K

Kapurthala, Maharada Jagatjit Singh of *73, 73*
Kawamata, Tadashi 289, *294*
Kim, Youngjun 195

Klipfel, Céline *136*
Kluge, Leon *113*, 242
Kongjian, Yu 242, 256, *256*
Konrads, Cornelia 282, 289
Kurkdjian, Francis 225, 242

L
Labat, Pierre *128*
Lacoste, Romain *196*
Laitinen, Antti *312*, *312*
Lamoureux, Julien *231*
Lang, Jack *107*
Langel, Frédéric *180*
Lapie, Christian 289, *294*
Laport, Stefan *149*, *226*
Larinier, Frédérique *118*
Laure, Johan *206*
Lavaud, Pierre *210*
Law, Rebecca Louise *158*, 282, 289
Le Brun, Charles 43
Le Dantec, Jean-Pierre *178*
Le Dantec, Tangi *178*
Le Gal, Laure *195*
Le Gourrièrec, Stéphane *127*
Le Merdy, Hélène *174*
Le Ray de Chaumont, Jacques-Donatien 19, 71, 81
Le Ray de Chaumont, James 57
Le Yondre, Yann *183*
Lebrun, Charles 43
Lecomte, Sophie *221*
Leduc, Dimitri *180*
Lehanneur, Mathieu *81*, 242, 244, 282, 289
Lehec, Alexandre *187*
Lemmonier, Kevin *187*
Lenzlinger, Jörg *277*, 282, 289
Lepage, Victor *187*
Leroux, Caroline *136*
"Lessive en fleurs" (2009) *149*, 215
Letellier, Jean-Michel *174*
Leurent, Paul *196*
Levallard, Jérôme *221*
"Levant" (2017) 225
Levêque de Vilmorin, Arthur *196*
Levy, Alexandre *221*
"Liberté, Égalité, Fraternité" (2012) *231*
Liebe, Sandra *215*
Lien infini (2016) *302*
"Livre de Sable, Le" (2018) *205*
"Locus genii, le génie est partout" (2012) *163*
Lorber, H. *149*, *226*
Loriers, Marie-Christine *144*, *150*
Louis XII (born Louis d'Orléans) 20, 22, *22*, 24, *24*
Louis XV, King of France 71, *71*

Louis XVI, King of France 19, 71, *71*
"Lucy in the Sky" (2011) *187*, *188*
Luquet, Camille *136*

M
"Ma cassette" (2014) *136*, *136*, *174*, 231
Ma terre, mater (2010) *154*, *154*, 205, 225
Macé, Charlotte *178*
Magnan, Julien *133*
Mahieu, Julie *120*
"Main dans la main" (2010) *154*, *154*
"Maison vivante, La" (2016) *187*
Manfredi, Fabio *215*
Marchalot, Christophe *163*
Marcion, Pierre Benoît 61
Margotin, Antoine 52
Marguerite, Queen of France (known as "La Reine Margot") 26
Marie-Antoinette 71, *71*
Marq, Pascale *183*
Martin, Chloé *116*
Martin, Jeanne *133*
Masanell, Franck *133*
Masillo, Antonietta *113*
Méchain, François 282, *312*, *318*
Medici, Catherine de' 16, 19, 26, *26*, 29, 32, *32*, 43, 46
Medici, Lorenzo de' 26
Meinrad, Luc *180*
Mercier, Florence 242
"Metempsychosis" (2010) *108*
Michel, Coralie *133*
Michel, Frédérique *180*
Millepied, Benjamin *154*, *154*, 242
Monet, Claude *166*
"Monochrome blanc" (2017) *215*
Montagne, Johanès *234*
Montefoschi, Carlotta *136*
Montel, Pascal *144*, *150*
Moonwalklocal, collective *205*
Morales, Ana *200*

N
Nakamura, Miki *174*
Nakaya, Fujiko *284*, 289
Napoleon 57
Nash, David *304*
Negron, Maud *120*
"Néo-Noé" (2016) *122*
Neto, Ernesto 242
Nid des murmures, Le (2017) 282, *282*
Nils-Udo *270*, 282
Nini, Giovanni Battista 19, 71, *71*
Nostradamus 26

Nouvellon, Guillaume *133*
"Nuances" (2015) *127*, *128*

O
Objets sphériques (2017) *307*
"Ocre Loire" (2009) 200, *200*
Orleans y Bourbon, Luis Fernando de 19
Orléans, Charles I 24, *24*
Orlov, Nicolas *81*, *83*
Orozco, Gabriel *10*, 282
Ortoli, Solène *239*
Oulipo 244

P
Panien, Étienne *107*
"Papillonnez" (2017) 234
"Paradis inversé" (2014) *187*, *187*, 215
"Paradis terrestre, Le" (2012) 144
"Parfums du vignoble, Les" (2013) *141*
Park, Sung Hye *133*
Pasquer, Claude *122*
Passard, Alain *108*, 242
Pastoureau, Michel *108*
Paysagistes sans Frontières, collectif *205*
Pelt, Jean-Marie *108*
Péna, Christine *187*
Péna, Michel *187*, 242
Penone, Giuseppe *270*
Pernet-Mugnier, Rémi *178*
Perrault, Charles 234
Perrault, Dominique 242
Petite Loire (2016) *81*, *244*, 282, 289
Pétrarque 22
Pezet, Guillaume *107*
Pheulpin, Simone 289
"Phoenix" (2016) *122*
Pichore, Jean 22
Pieran, Gianluca *215*
Pierre, Baptiste *183*
Pierres et le Printemps, Les (2015) *277*, 289
Pigeat, Jean-Paul *107*
Pillot, Laurène *128*
Pinault, Maryvonne *108*
Pinter, Klaus *81*, 282, 289, 304, *304*
Pivot, Bernard *108*
"Planète en ébullition, La" (2017) *171*, *171*
Plessix, Laurence du *183*
Poirée-Ville, Jean-Philippe *122*, *158*, *158*, *183*
Poirier, Anne *100*, *101*, 242, 289
Poirier, Patrick *100*, *101*, 242, 289
Poitiers, Diane de 16, 19, 29, *29*, 46, *46*

Polissky, Nicolay 289, *299*
"Pollen exubérant, Le" (2011) *174*, *174*
Pontet, Gérard *122*
"Porte-bonheur" (2015) *127*, *128*, 210
Poulenc, Francis 64
"Pour l'amour de Tongariro" (2014) *163*, *166*
"Pouvoir des sorcières, Le" (2017) *133*, *133*, 234
Prulière, Louise *231*
Puybonnieux, Emmanuel *118*

Q
Qasar Design University, collective *215*
"Quand l'avare rêve" (2014) *136*
"Que vienne la pluie" (2016) *118*, *122*, *158*, *190*, *195*

R
Racine, Michel 242
Racines de la Loire, Les (2014) 289, *299*
Ramalinghom, Fabrice *231*
Rebecchini, Luigi *136*
Récamier, madame 57
"Recto-verso" (2009) *149*
"Réflexion d'un collectionneur" (2015) *166*, *239*
"Réflexion faite" (2018) *215*
"Réflexions" (2009) *163*
Reinoso, Pablo 242, 289, *294*
Renard, Armelle *171*
Renoir, Auguste *166*
"Résurrection, éloge de la défaillance" (2014) *200*, *200*, 215
"Rêve de Pantagruel, Le" (2010) 154
Reymbouts, Martin 44
Ribstein, Marguerite *192*
Richardson, George *108*
Ripoche, Michaël *174*
"Rivière des sens, La" (2013) *163*, *168*
Rivière, Étienne *144*
Robin, Christophe 242
Rothschild family 64
Rouvillois, Jonathan *231*
Rouxel, Julie *239*
Ruggieri, Cosimo 26, *26*, 29, *29*, 30
Rydingsvard, Ursula von 289, *318*

S
Saccharumania (2017) *41*
Samakh, Erik *228*, 289
Sanson, Paul-Ernest 19, 52, 54, 64, 81, *81*

Santacreu Felis, Anna *171*
Sante, Simone *215*
Sardi, Samuel *215*
Sarkis *10*
Sartre, Éric *116*
Saumur, Ingrid *231*
"Saute qui peut!" (2013) *231*
Say, Marie-Charlotte-Constance (see also Broglie, Princess de) 19, 29, 64, 95
Schlegel, Wilhelm 57
Schrader, Sarah *221*
Schubert, Armin 289, 304, *307*
"Sculptillonnage" (2011) *118*, 122
"Sens dessus dessous" (2018) *310*
Serreau, Coline *9*, 108
Shu, Wang *171*, 242, 256, 261, *261*
Sicard, Louis *171*
"Silence ! Ça mousse" 127
Simon, Jacques 242
Simon, Olivier *141*
Simonson, David *210*
"Sniffettes" (2013) 225
Solario, Andrea 22
Sorre, Tanguy *178*
"Soulèvement des graines, Le" (2016) *196*
Springeling, Jasper *221*
Stadler, Alice *218*
Stadler, Nicolas *218*
Staël, Germaine de (born Germaine Necker, Baronness de Staël-Holstein) 16, 57, *57*, 61, *61*
Steiner, Gerda *277*, 282, 289
Strootman, Berno *221*
Suissa, Nicolas *168*
"Suspensions climatiques" (2015) *174*, *180*, 190, 195
Suzuki, Shodo 262, *262*
Szwed, Pauline *188*

T
Taillard, Emmanuel *183*
Takano, Fumiaki *249*, 262
Tanguy, Claire *231*
Tasselli, Giulia *215*
"Temple de nos pensées, Le" (2018) *195*
"The Archipelago" (2013) 262, *262*
Thomas, Olivier *144*
Tito, Santi di 26
"Toi et moi, une rencontre" (2012) 225, *225*
Tollu, Béatrice *144*, *150*

Tour d'Auvergne, Madeleine de la 26
Tricaud, Pierre-Marie *183*
Tricoire, Alexis *171*, *171*, 282
"Trône de fleurs, Le" (2017) 231

U
"Ugwu" (2017) *309*, 312
"Ultraviolet" (2014) 174
"Un paysage à goûter" (2013) *183*, *183*

V
Valentini, Aurelio *215*
Van den Berg, Richard *187*
Van der Hout, Arie *187*
"Vasques vives" (2008) 171
Verschueren, Bob 289
Viale, Amélie *215*
"Vilain Petit Jardin de Jean-Michel Vilain, Le" (2010) *231*
Villa Marcello, Christian *215*
Villanis Ziani, Maria Cecilia *136*
Villette, Clément *128*
Vinci, Leonardo da 22
Viviès, Cathy *166*
"Vivre au jardin" (2016) *205*, *205*
Vogel, Anouk *150*
"Voir les sons, entendre les couleurs" (2013) *141*, 163, *221*
"Voir rouge" (2009) *149*, *150*, 200
Volcan (2018) *270*, 282
Voltaire 71
"Voyage intérieur, Le" (2018) *178*
Vries, Herman de 289

W
Walsh, family 19, 50
Weiss, Laurent *154*
Willemsen, Matthijs *221*
Wirtz, Jacques *107*
Wolfensberger, Andrea 289, *289*
Würster, Joachim *149*, *226*

X
XiXe (2015) *309*, 312

Y
Yamou, Abderrahim 289, *302*
Yoro, Laura *144*
Yuanming, Tao 261
Yushmanova, Yekaterina *174*

Z
Zaragoza, Anna *221*
Zhou, Chen-Yu *234*

ACKNOWLEDGMENTS

The author offers warm thanks to Eric Sander for his remarkable photographs.
She would also like to express her gratitude to François Bonneau, President of the Region
of the Centre-Val de Loire, for his unwavering support, and to Bernard Faivre d'Arcier,
Chairman of the Board of Administration of the Domain of Chaumont-sur-Loire,
as well as to all the board members. Thanks, too, to the team at the Domaine for
their complete commitment to this extraordinary cultural adventure.
Specific thanks are due to Elizabeth Mettling and John Touchet for their
invaluable help in bringing this book to completion.
Thanks, too, to Suzanne Tise-Isoré, Editorial Director of Style & Design
at Flammarion, as well as to her team, Gwendoline Blanchard, Bernard Lagacé,
Lysandre le Cléac'h, and Lara Lo Calzo, for their contribution to the project.

PHOTOGRAPHIC CREDITS

FACING PAGE François Méchain, *L'Arbre aux échelles*
(The Tree with Ladders), 2009.
PAGE 320 Ursula von Rydingsvard, *Anastazia*, 2017.